WINTER

While fall is my favorite time of year with its riot of colors and cool autumn days, there is magic about winter, especially when snow covers our yard, and we get up in the morning to the sun shining over glistening trees and a snowy blanket. New snow sparkles like diamonds, and makes everything appear pristine. This is when we tend to forget about traffic jams, hazardous roads, and how much shoveling that needs to be done. Instead, we think about snowmen, sledding, and all the fun things that come with winter.

In this book, I've provided winter designs for tangling, and coloring, too. I hope you enjoy them and post them on Facebook so everyone can see how wonderful your work turned out.

We'll begin with the basics in setting up a tangle before moving into the designs and filling them with assorted tangles. Instead of a separate page of how-to step-outs, the tangle how-to's are placed near the designs to show how they have been done. The reasoning behind this is so readers won't have to flip back and forth to see how to do a tangle. This is for your convenience. Readers have spoken, and I listened when they did, so I do hope this is more helpful to you.

Occasionally, I blog about tangling, and give away free items or books. I also enjoy reading the comments left by everyone who stops by. It's nice to know what other tanglers are doing and to learn about their projects. My blog is: http://zenoftangling.blogspot.com

With that said, let's start tangling!!

Jeanne

SUPPLIES & STUFF

There are so many art supplies for sale these days that it boggles the mind. However, in Zentangle, the use of monochromatic colors, such as black and white, are the norm. A friend of mine once said that color makes you think by way of considering values, hues, what goes with what, and how to work the overall image out. With black and white, it becomes easier. Using a 3 1/2" square tile (piece of heavy paper) also lends itself to ease and less fear of a huge white sheet of paper that can be overwhelming to fill up. Begin simple and move on from there to build confidence before working larger. Small sketch books are perfect for beginners (and the more experienced tangler, too) because they can be carried with you for tangling whenever you have free time. A 3 1/2" square tile, a #2 pencil, and an 01 black Micron pen (or any waterproof pen) is all you need to get started.

To use color: watercolor pencils, colored pencils, markers, acrylic paint, gouache, Sakura pens, and brush pens are some of the materials easily used to add color to tangles. Be brave, "There are No Mistakes, Only Opportunities" with Zentangle®. Be happy with what you can accomplish and let that happiness replenish your inner artist. Tangling builds confidence in what you do!

My journey into Zentangle® began several years ago. I was hooked on this marvelous art form the moment I tried it, and I hope you will be, too. Tangling is good for people of all ages. Senior citizens, young children, teens and adults can benefit from tangling daily.

Have fun and ENJOY!!

Use the pencil to add a dot in each corner, and then draw a continuous line from one dot to the other, creating a square. Section it by placing a couple of lines inside as is tile #1. Use the pen to draw tangles, take time and if you have a Micron pen, try not to press hard on the tip as it will ruin the pen. Relax your hand and hold the pen lightly for more control.

#1 Use my tangle examples, or create some. Once the tangle is drawn, add shading using the pencil and smudge the lead with your fingertip to give the tangle depth.

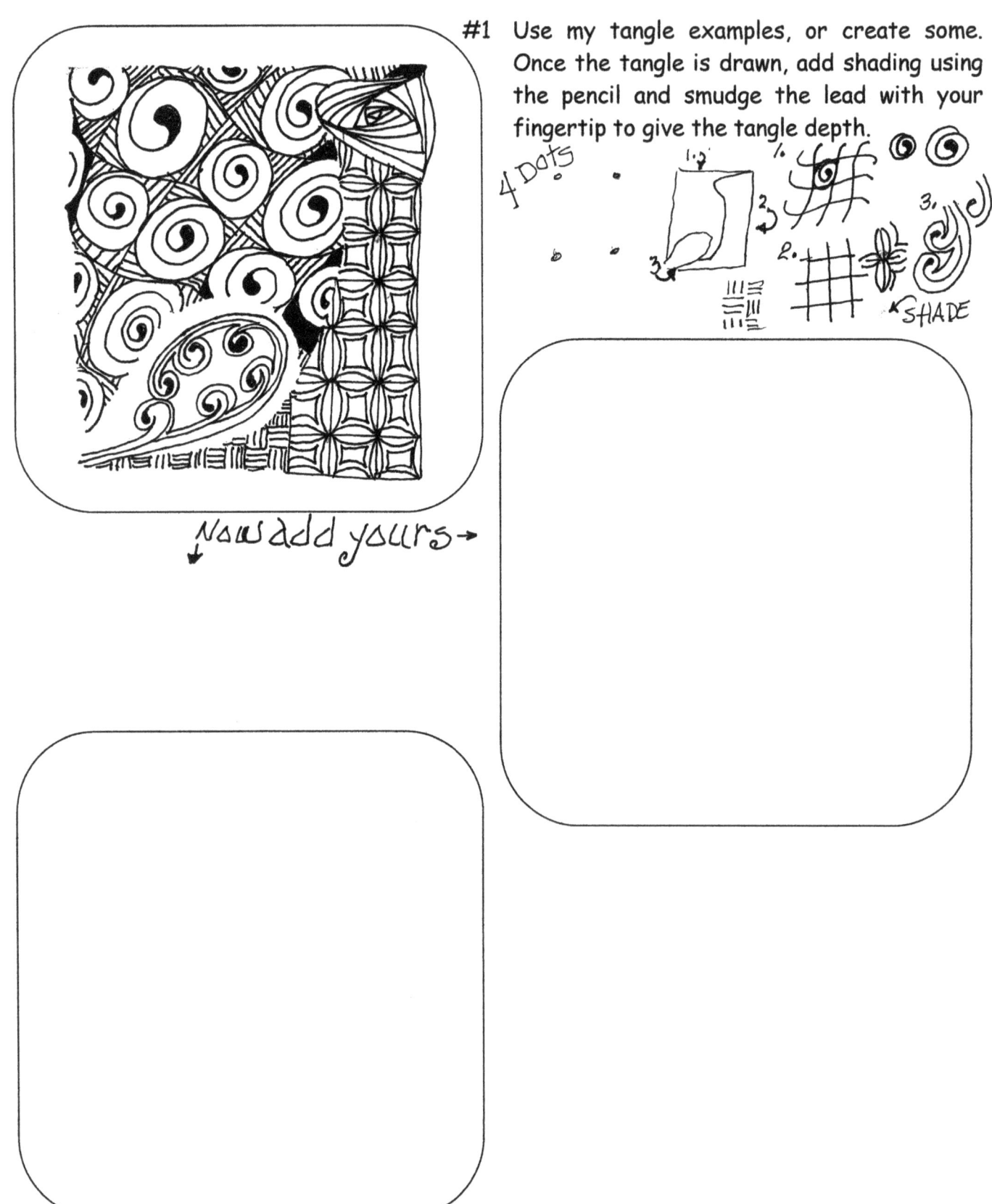

Now add yours →

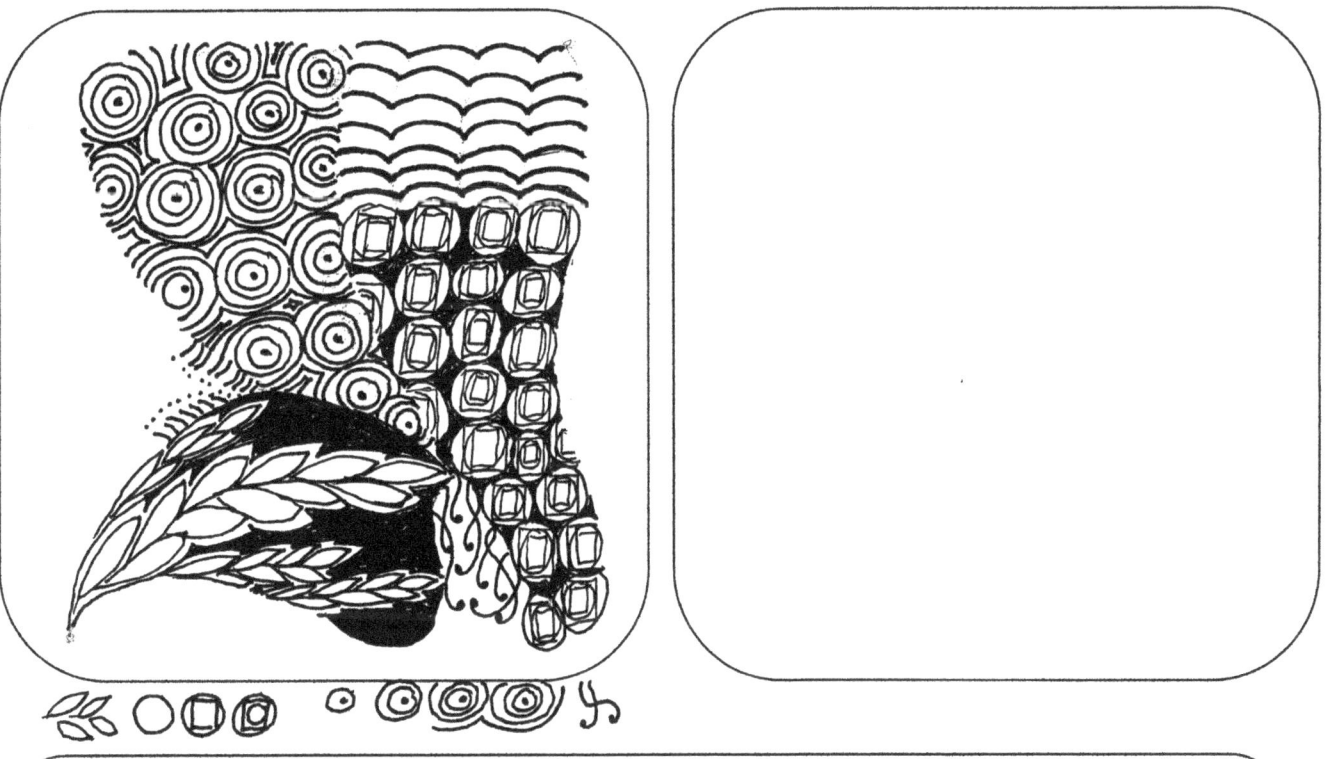

There are no Mistakes in Zentangle.
There are Only Opportunities . . .

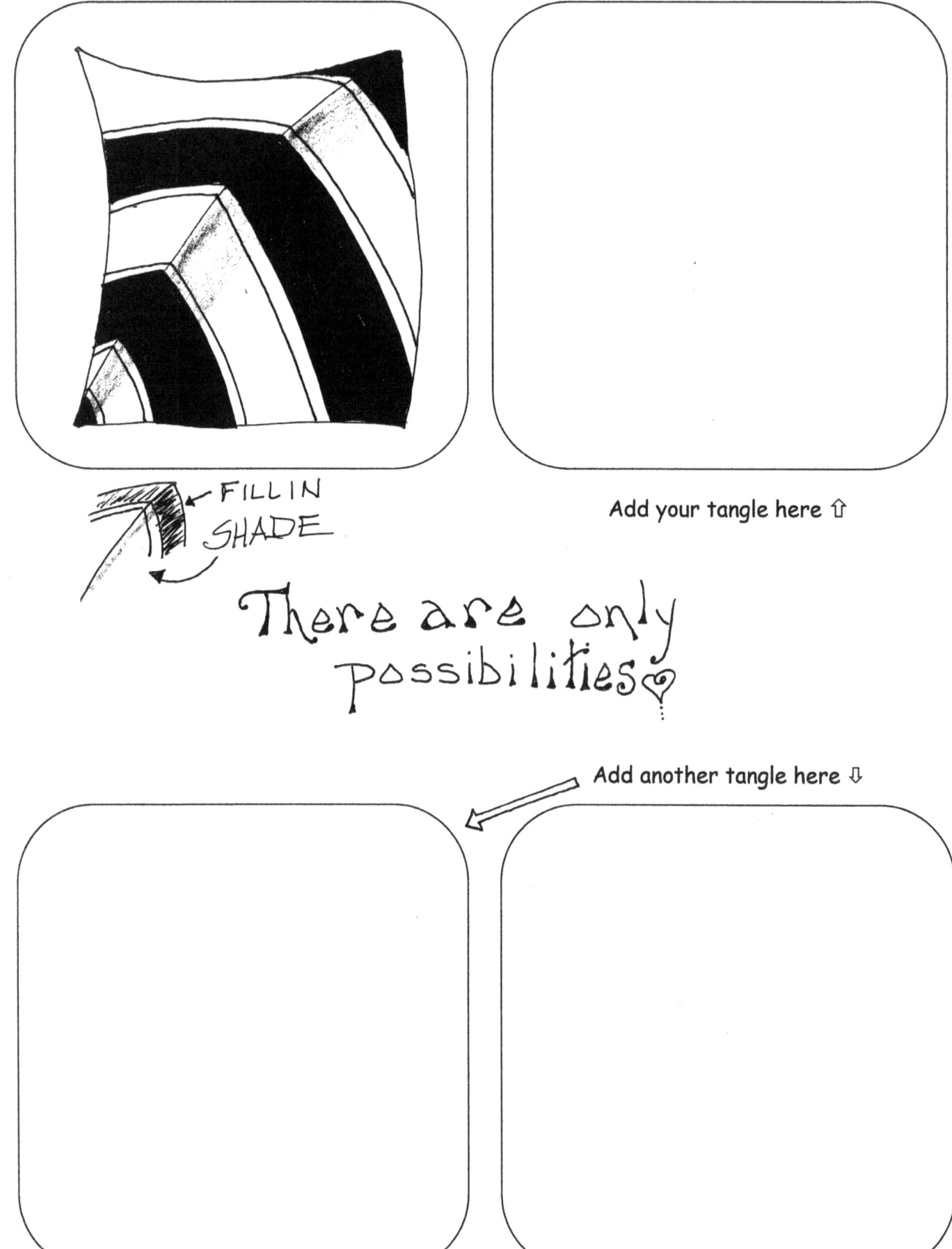

FILL IN
SHADE

Add your tangle here ⇧

There are only
possibilities♡

Add another tangle here ⇩

✐ Note how you configured your tangles.

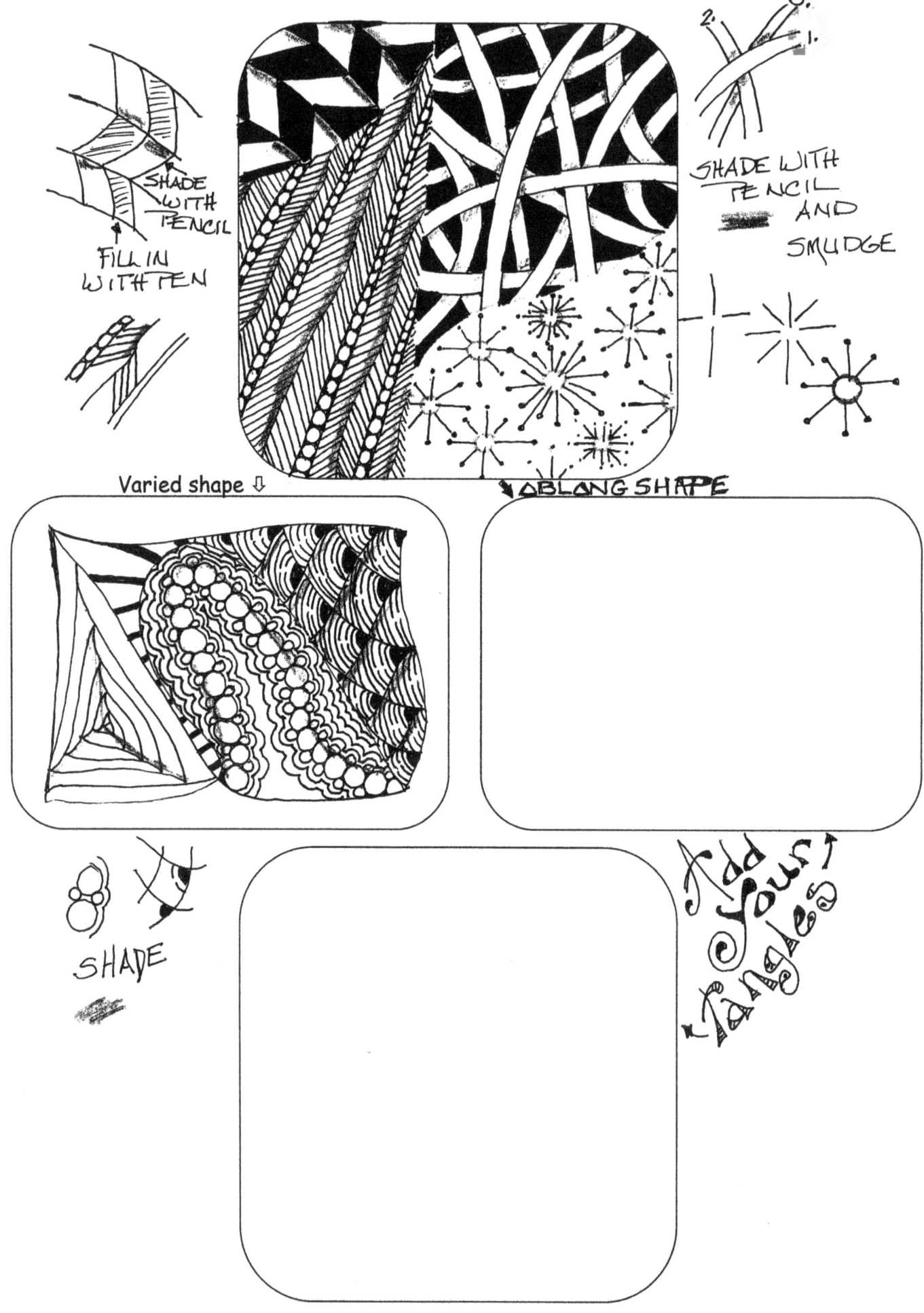

SHADE WITH PENCIL

FILL IN WITH PEN

SHADE WITH PENCIL AND SMUDGE

Varied shape ⇩

OBLONG SHAPE

SHADE

Add Your Tangles

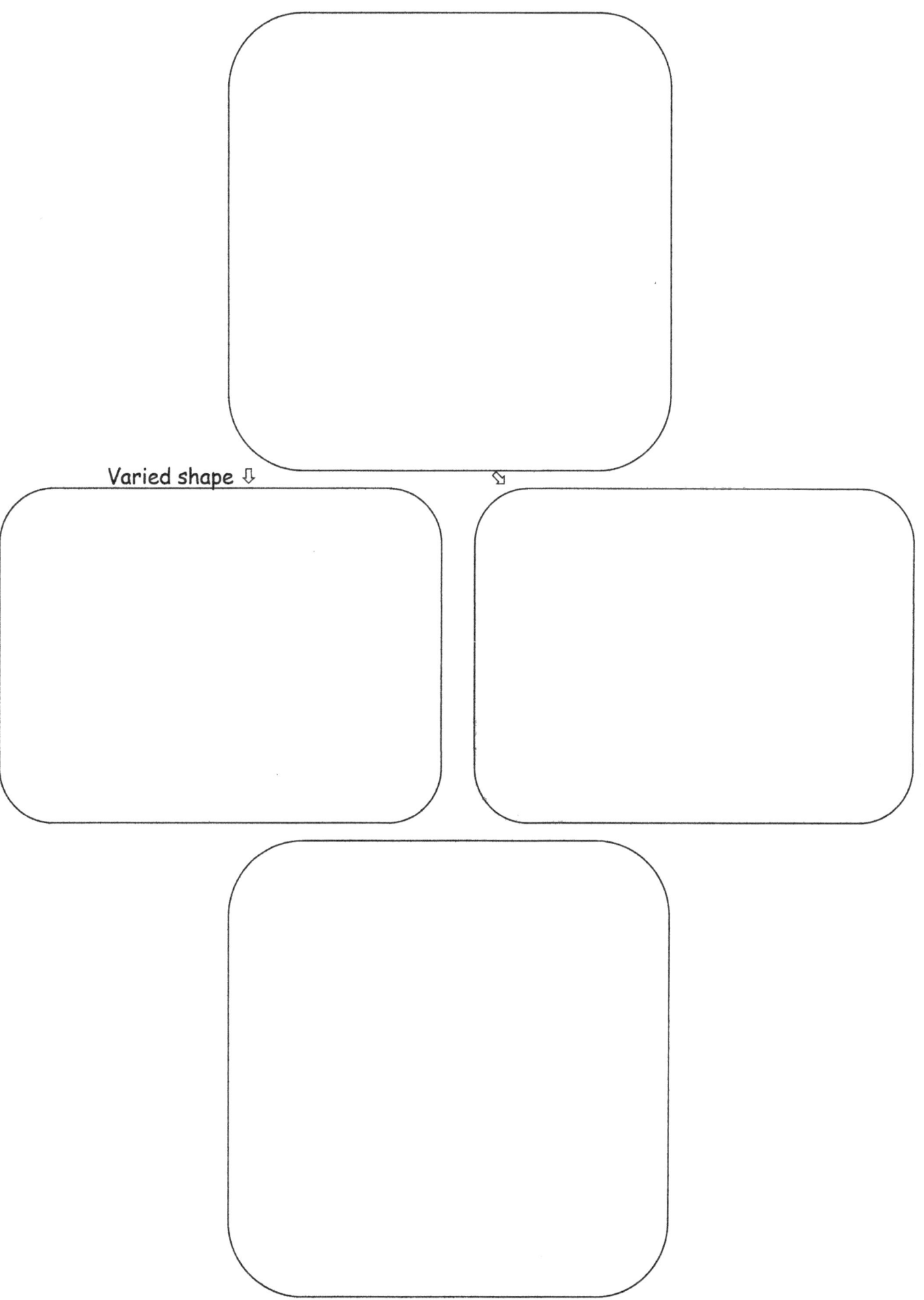

Varied shape ⇩   ⇖

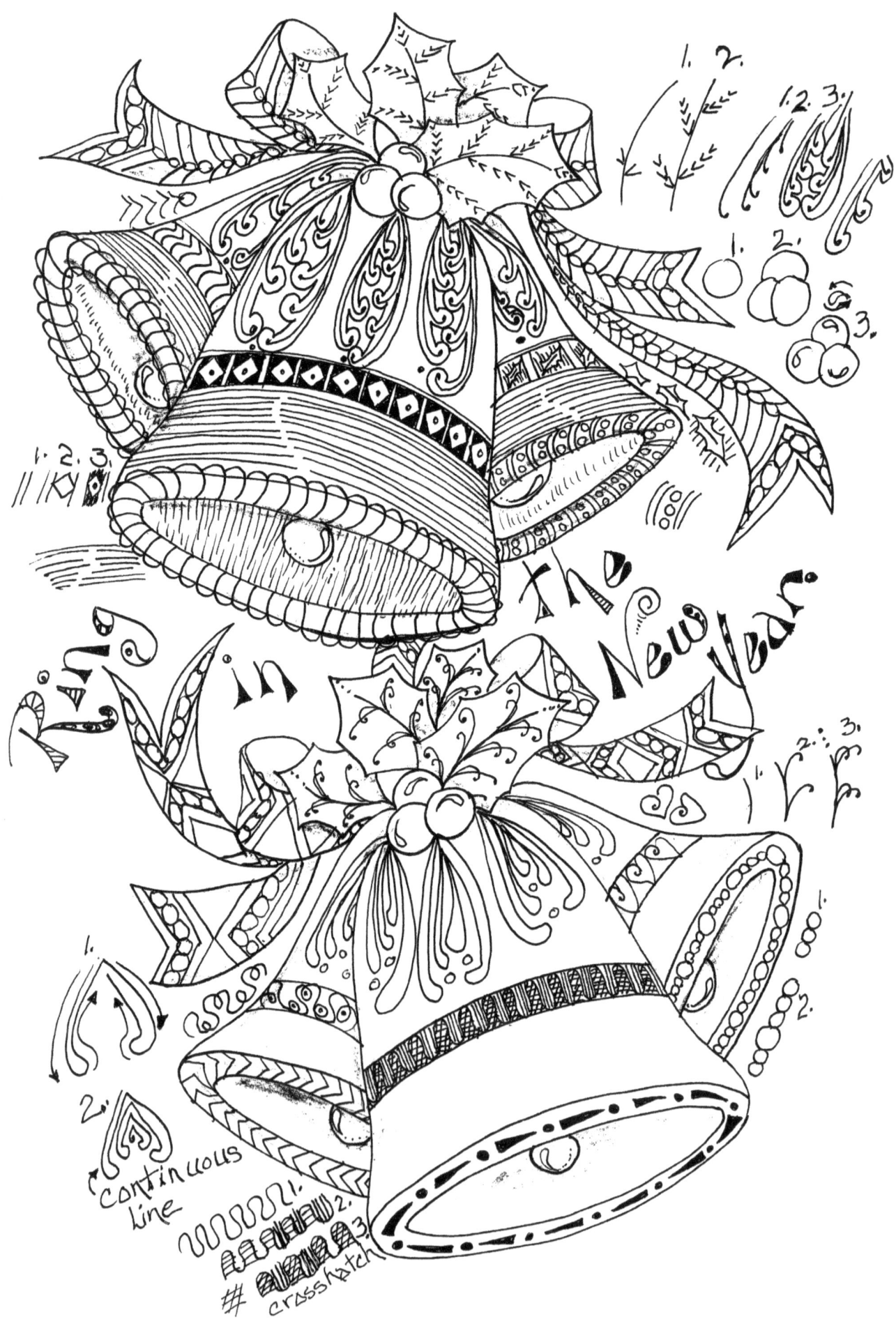

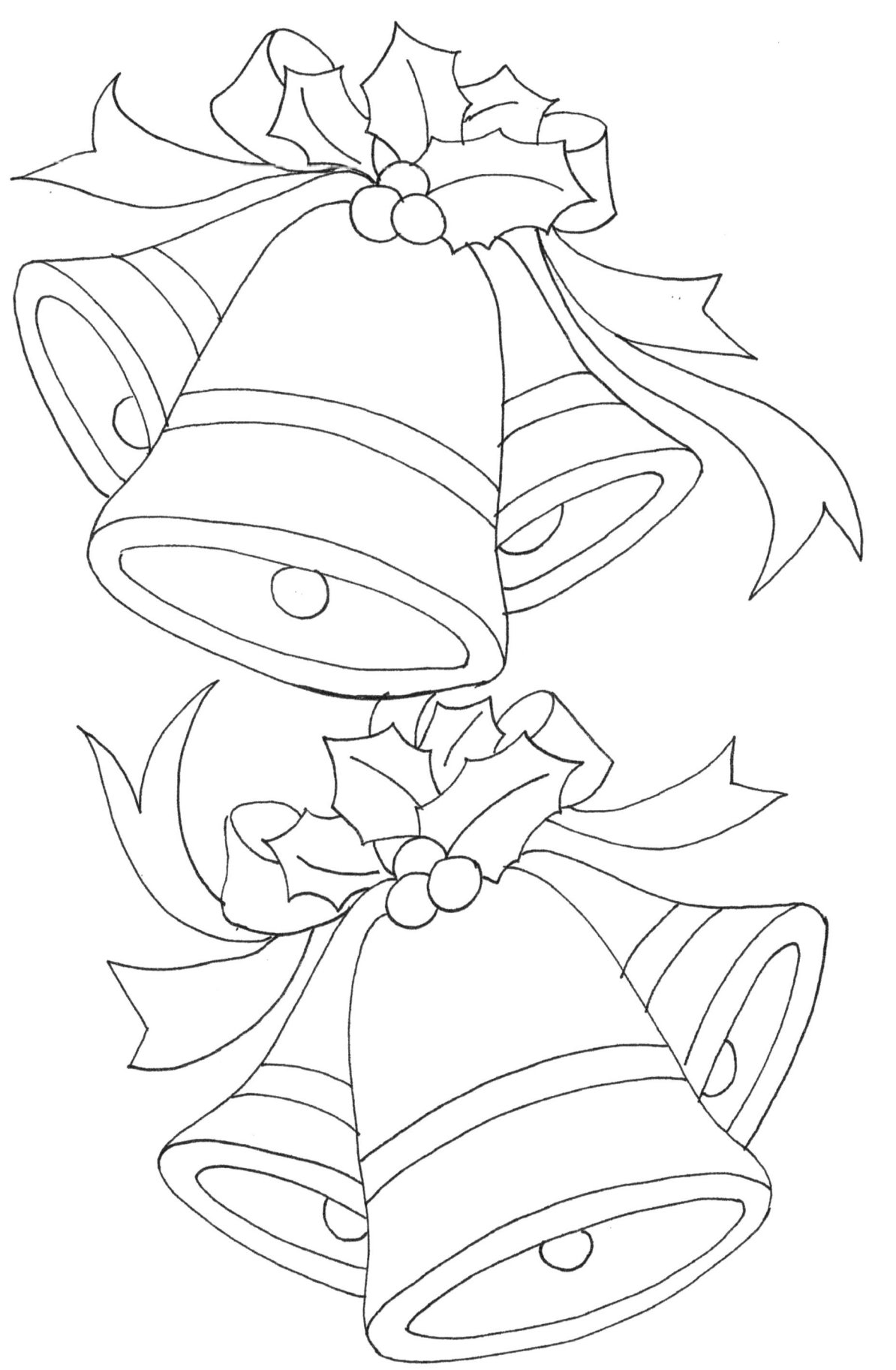

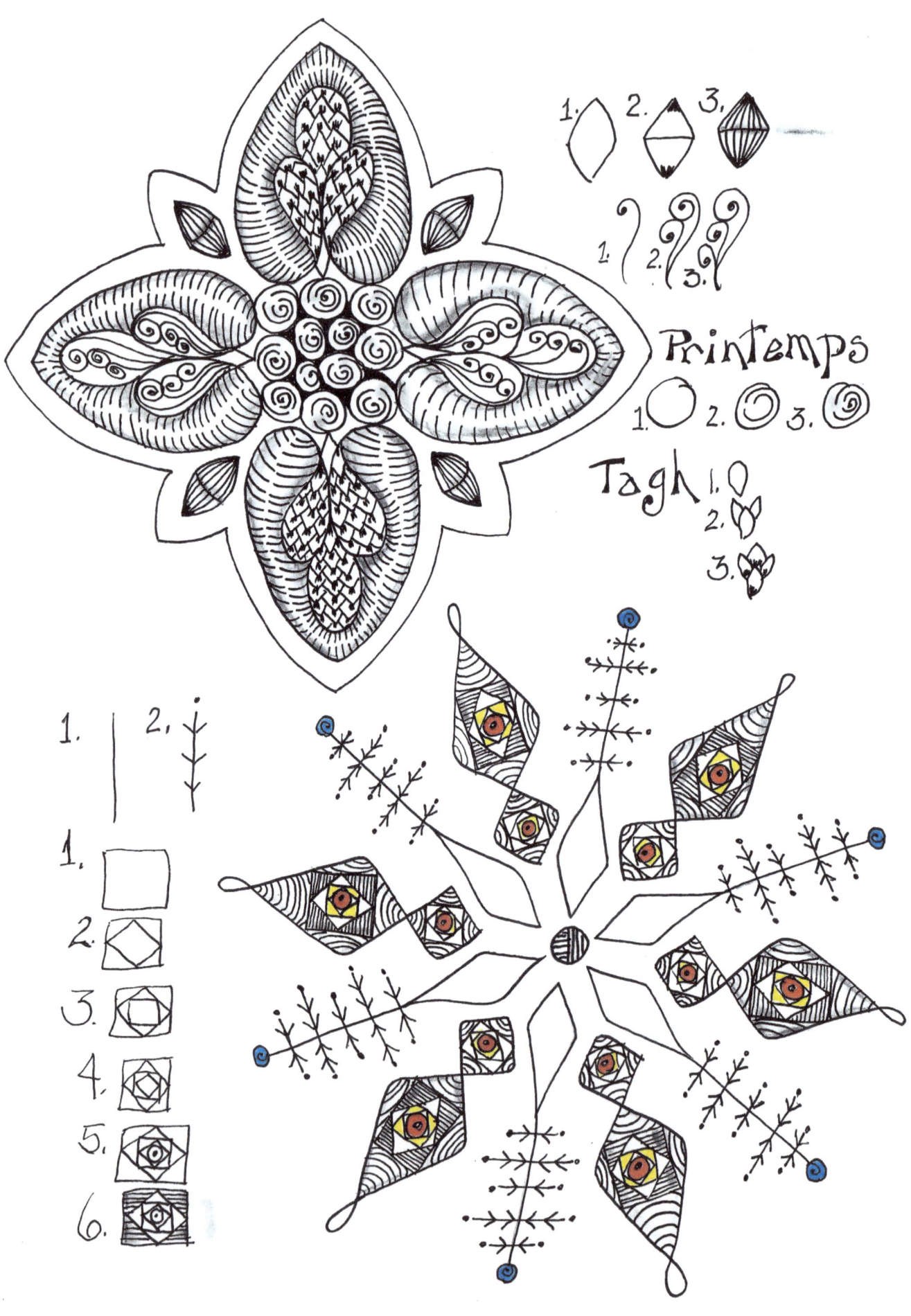

1. 2. 3.

1. 2. 3.

Printemps
1. 2. 3.

Tagh
1.
2.
3.

1. | 2.

1.
2.
3.
4.
5.
6.

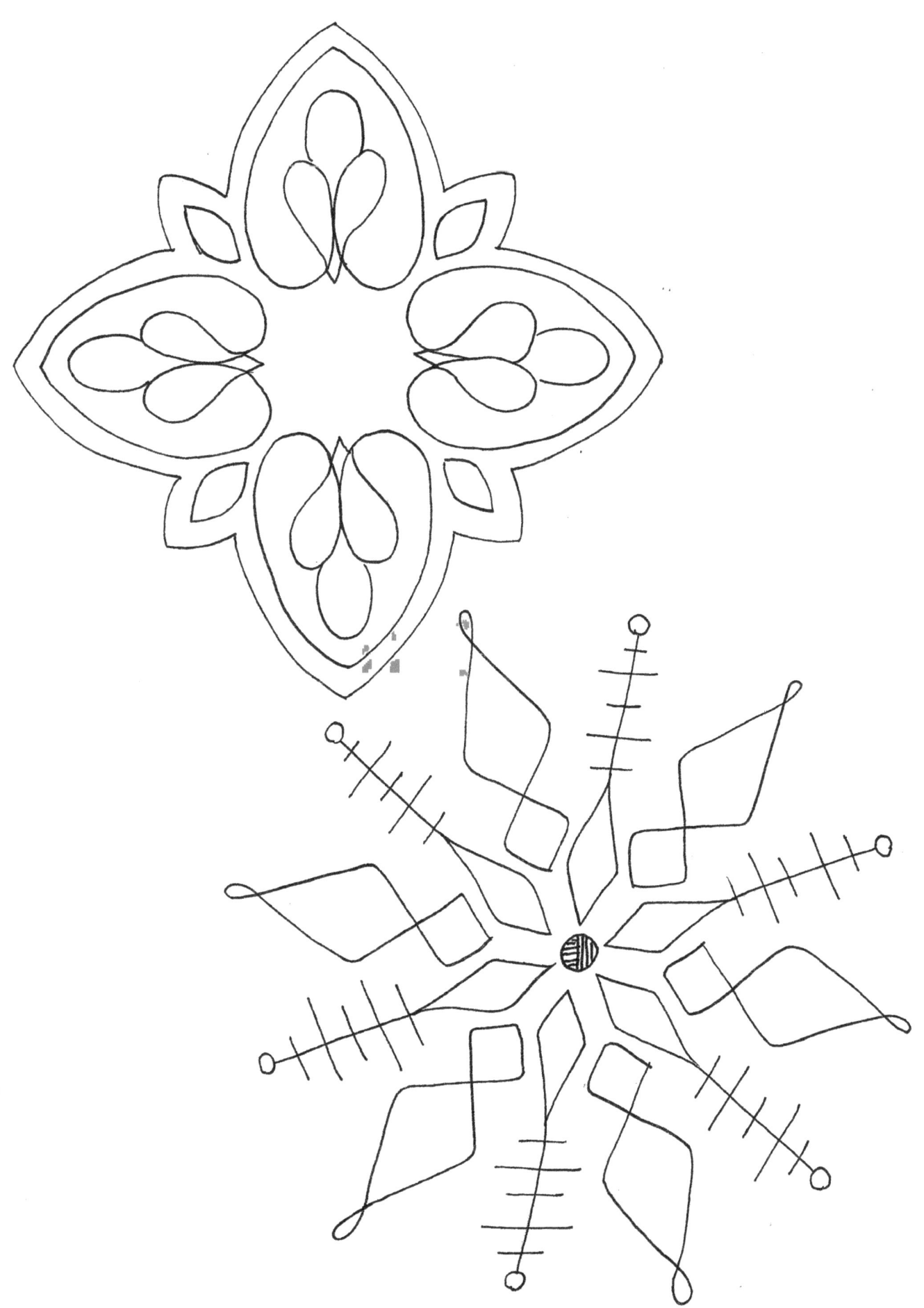

An exercize
for you.

#1

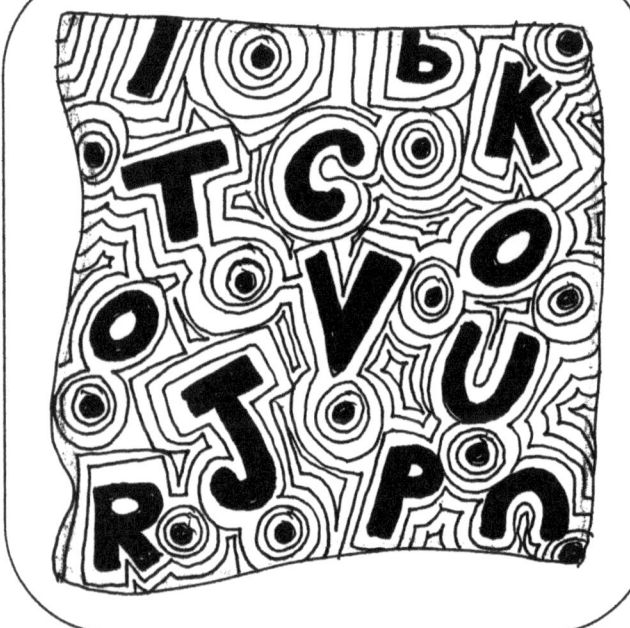

#2

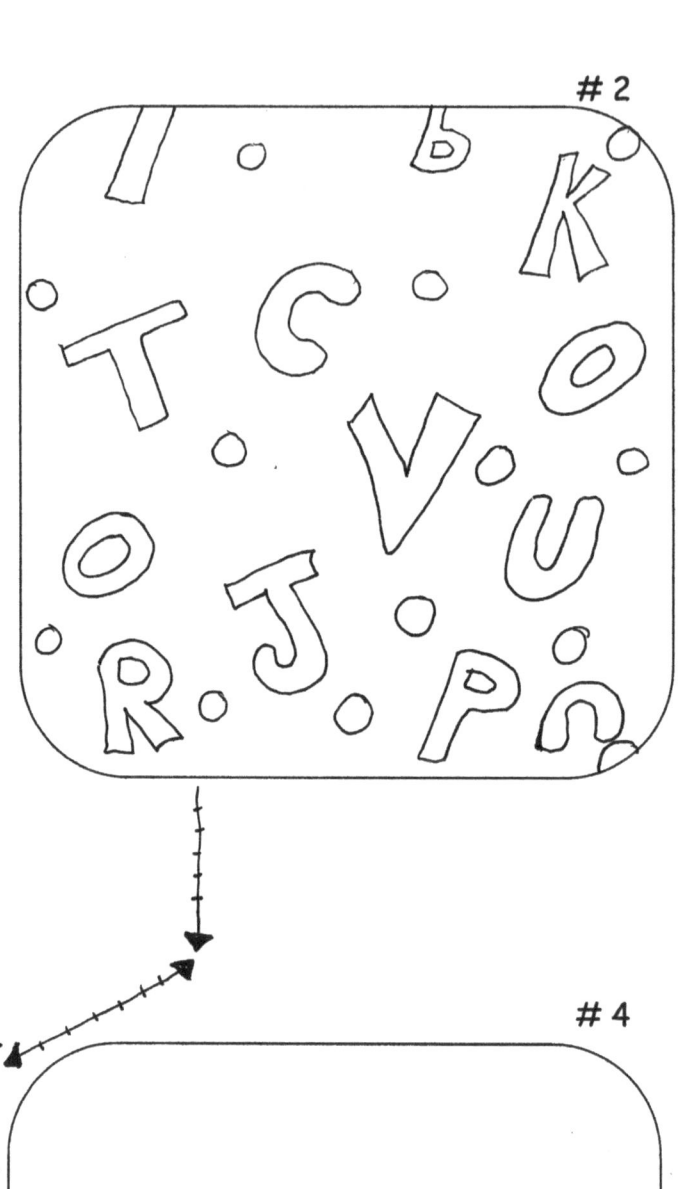

Be mindful
of your marks!

Shade last

REPEAT

#3

#4

Breathe, Relax,
Sit back
& smile.

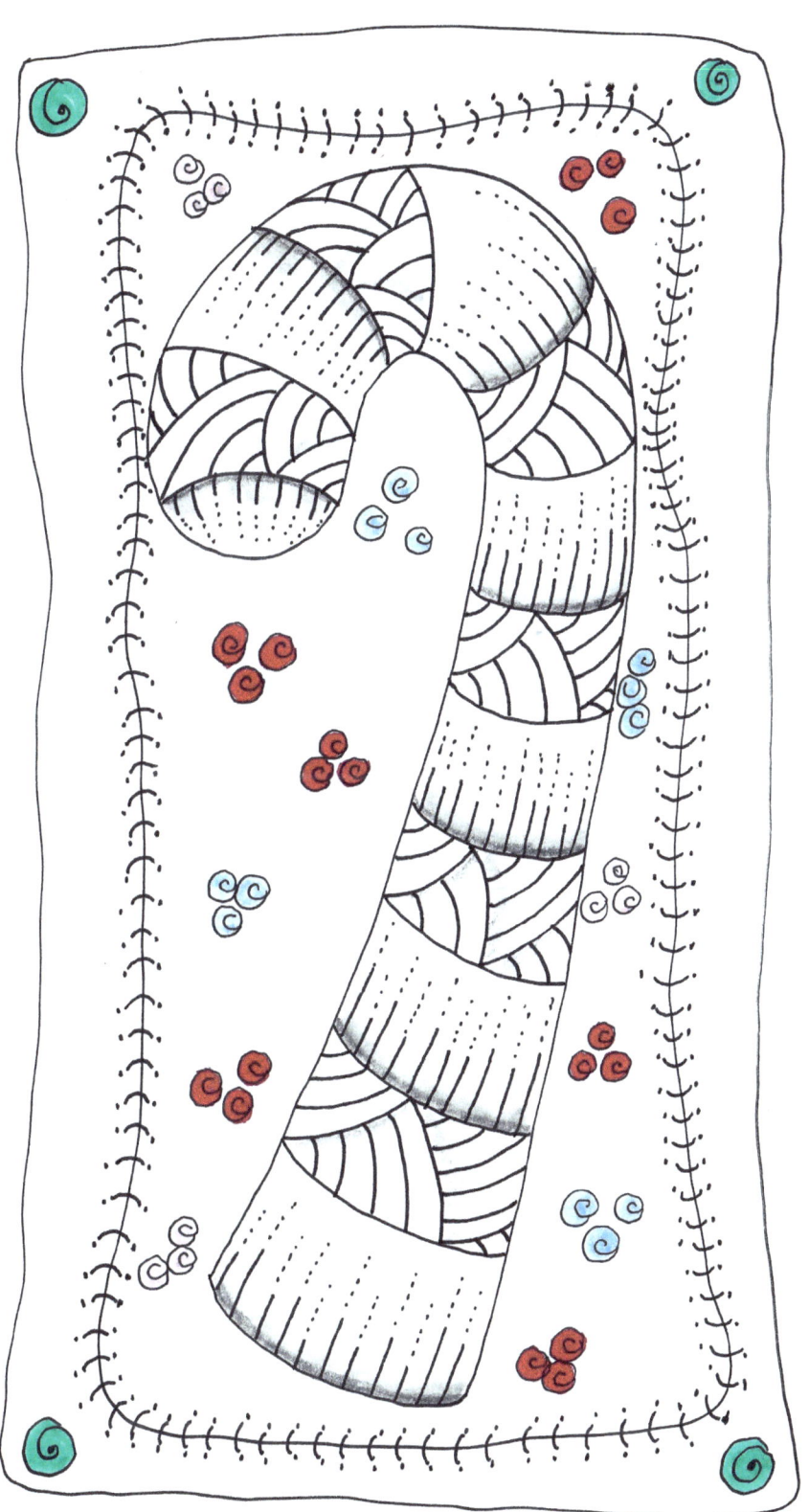

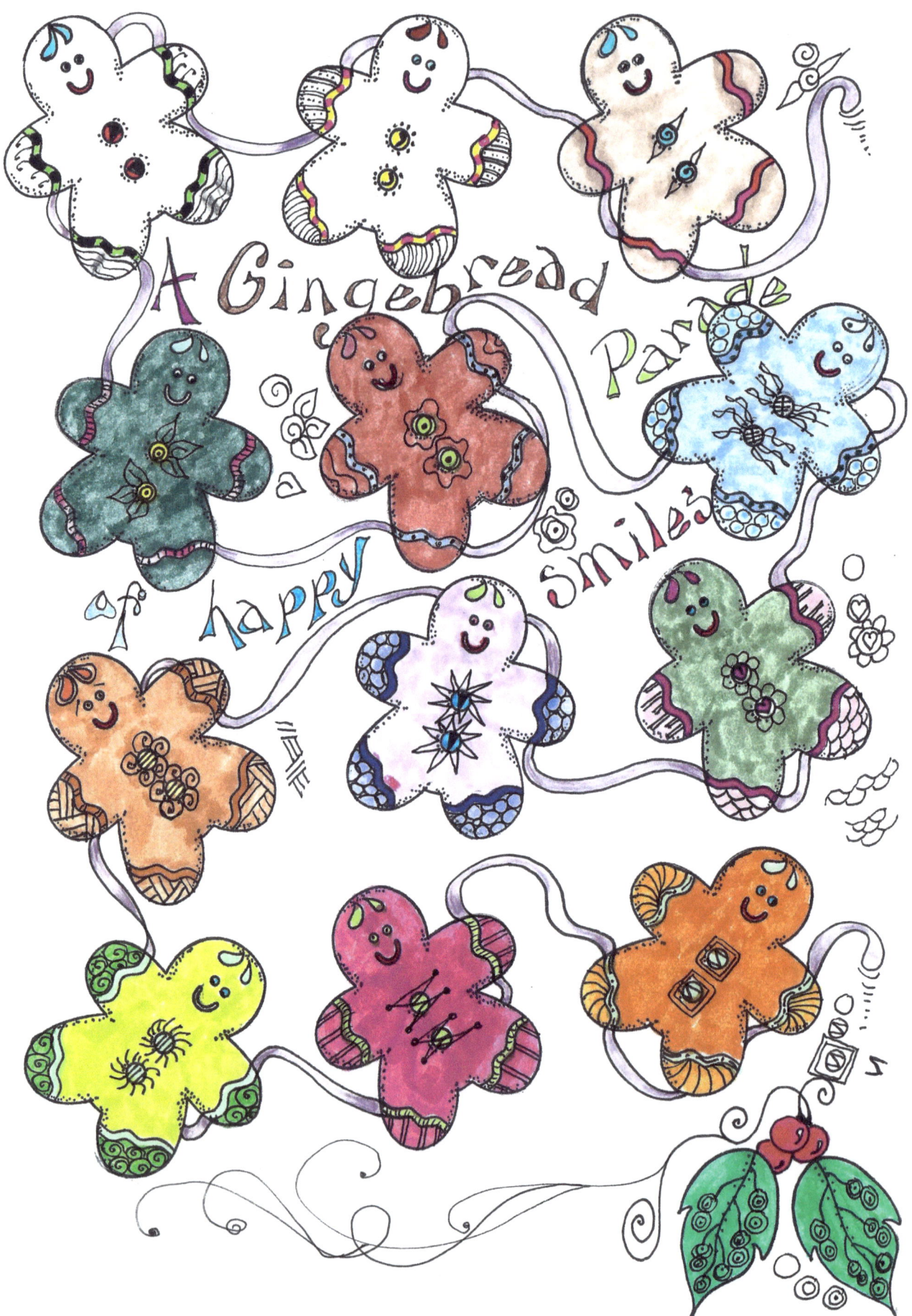

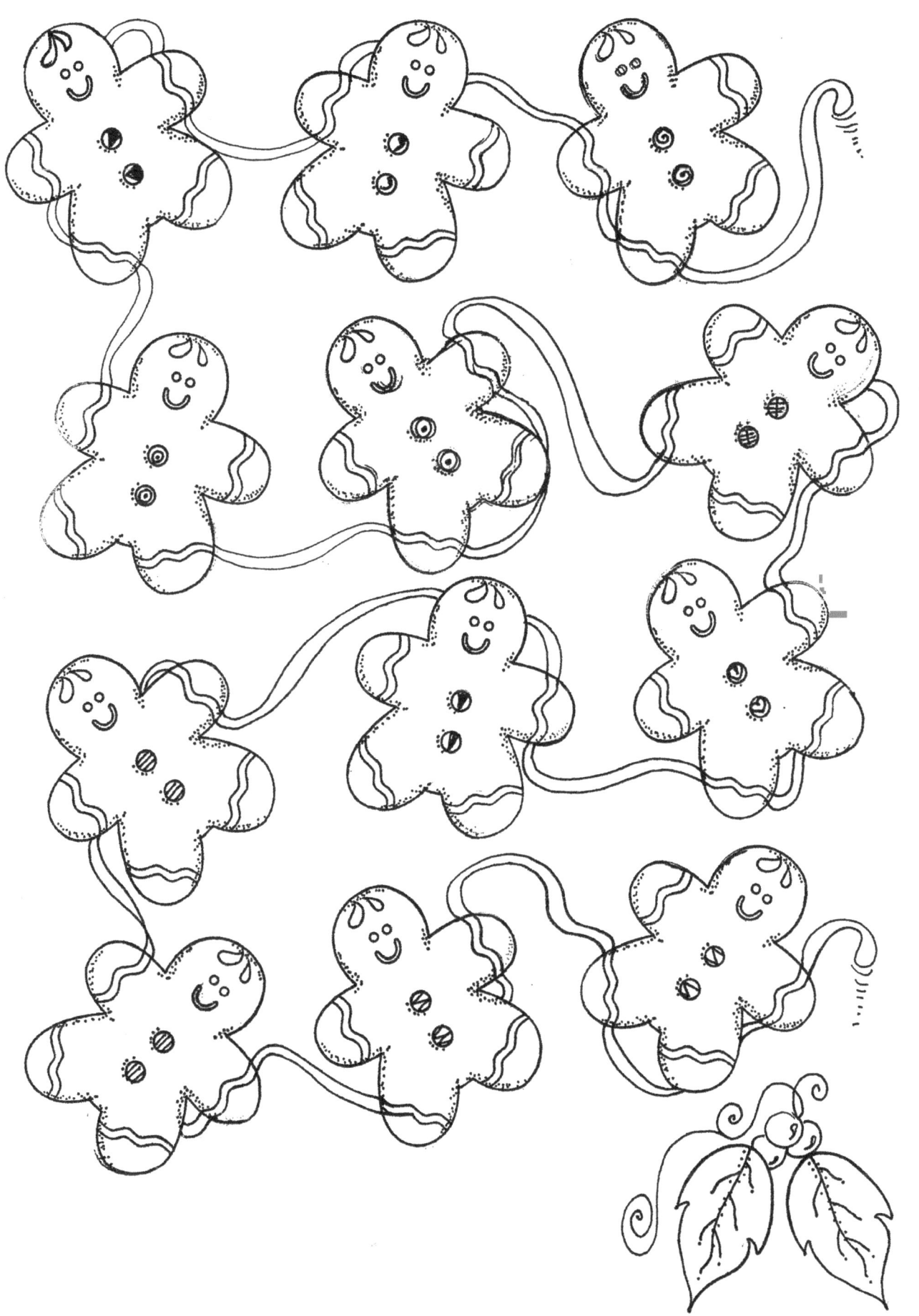

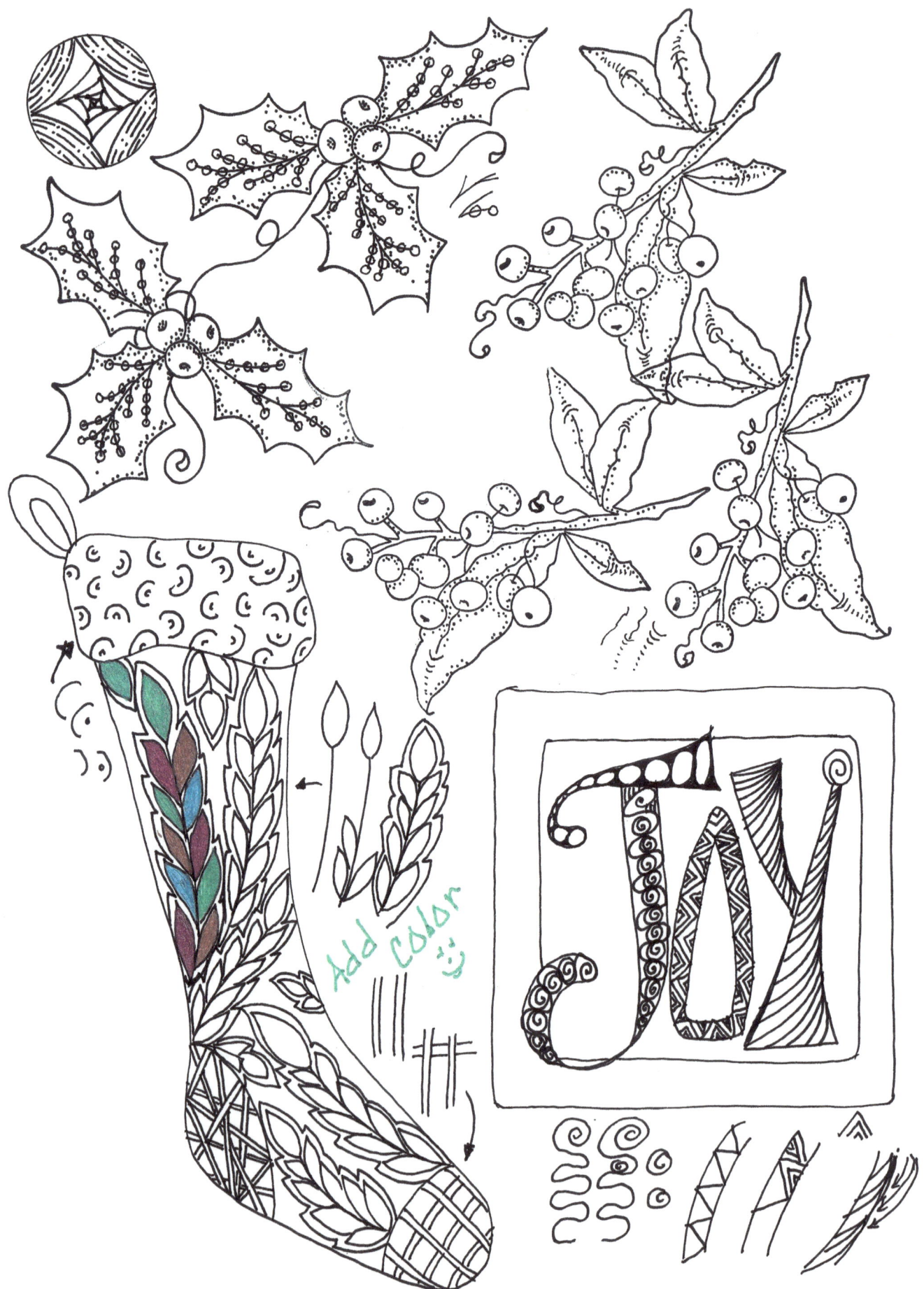

Add Color ☺

JOY

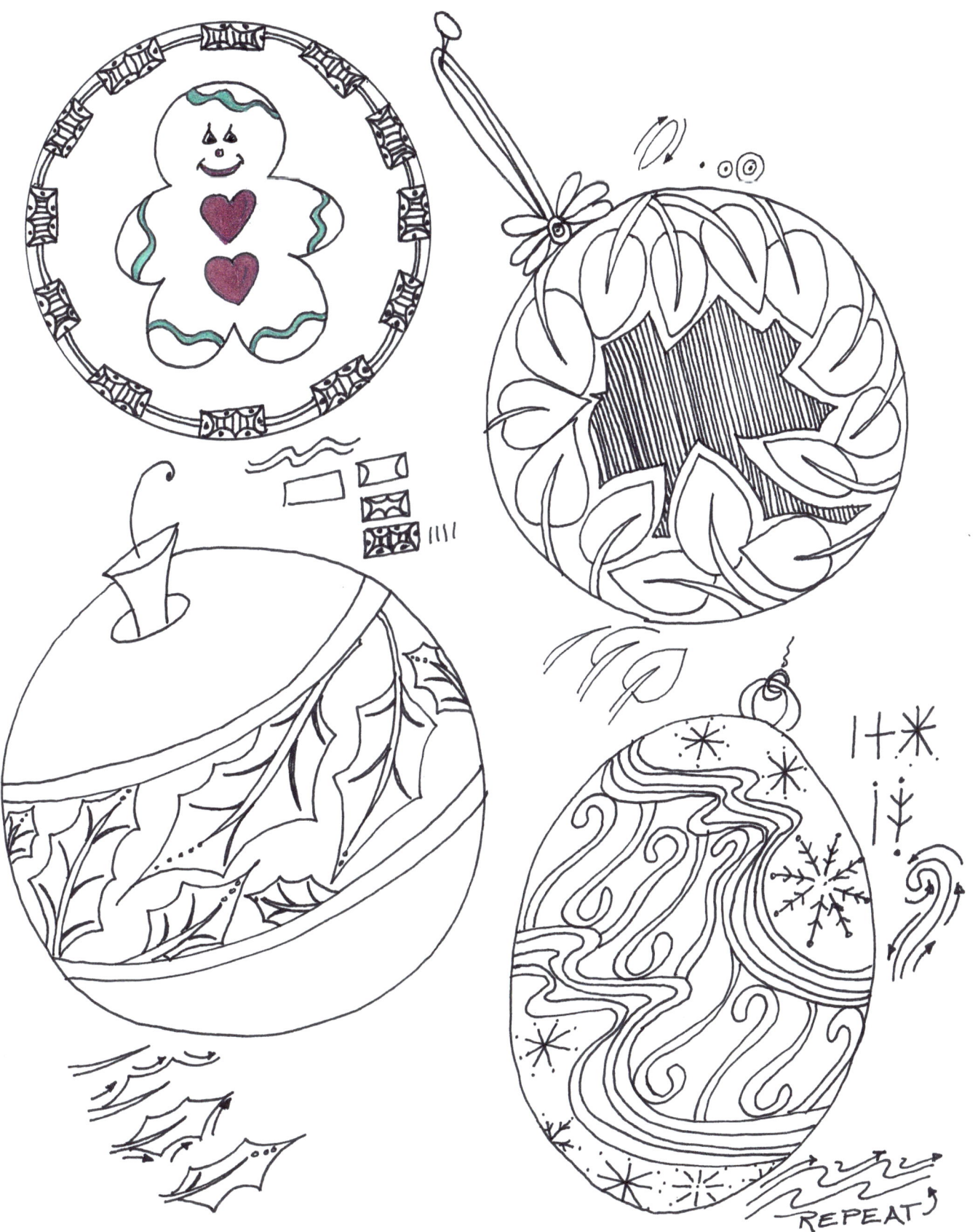

REPEAT

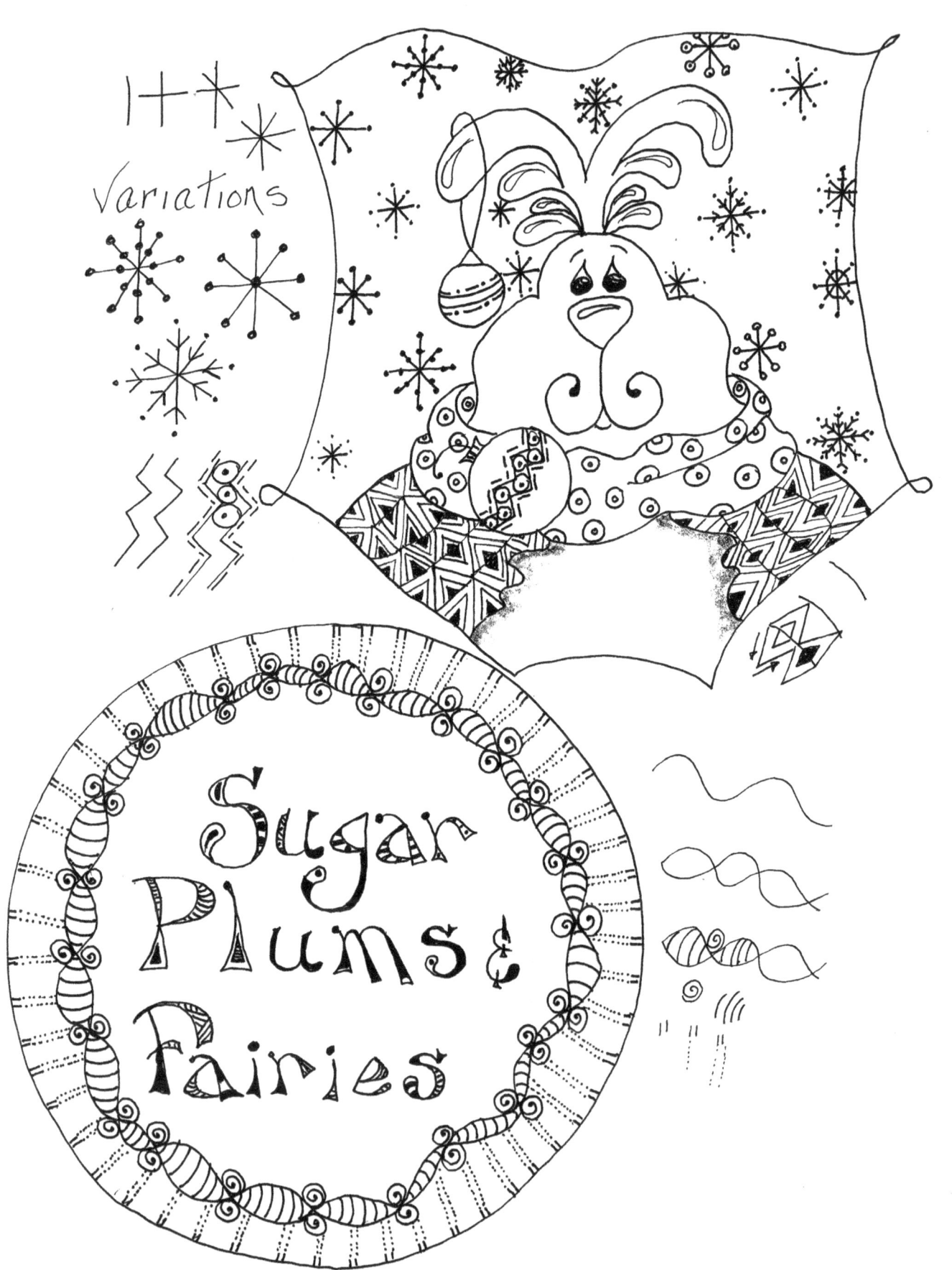

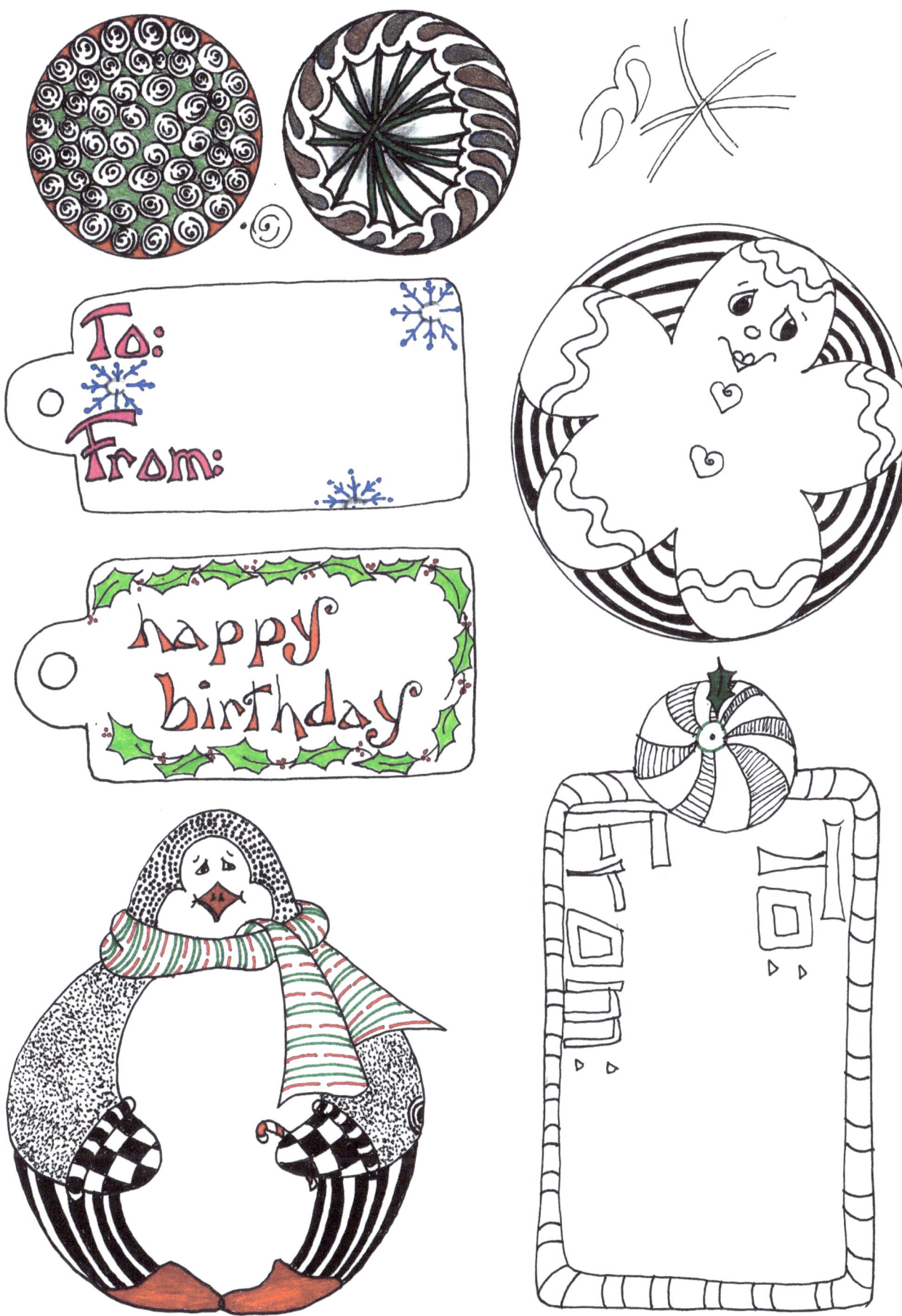

To:

From:

happy birthday

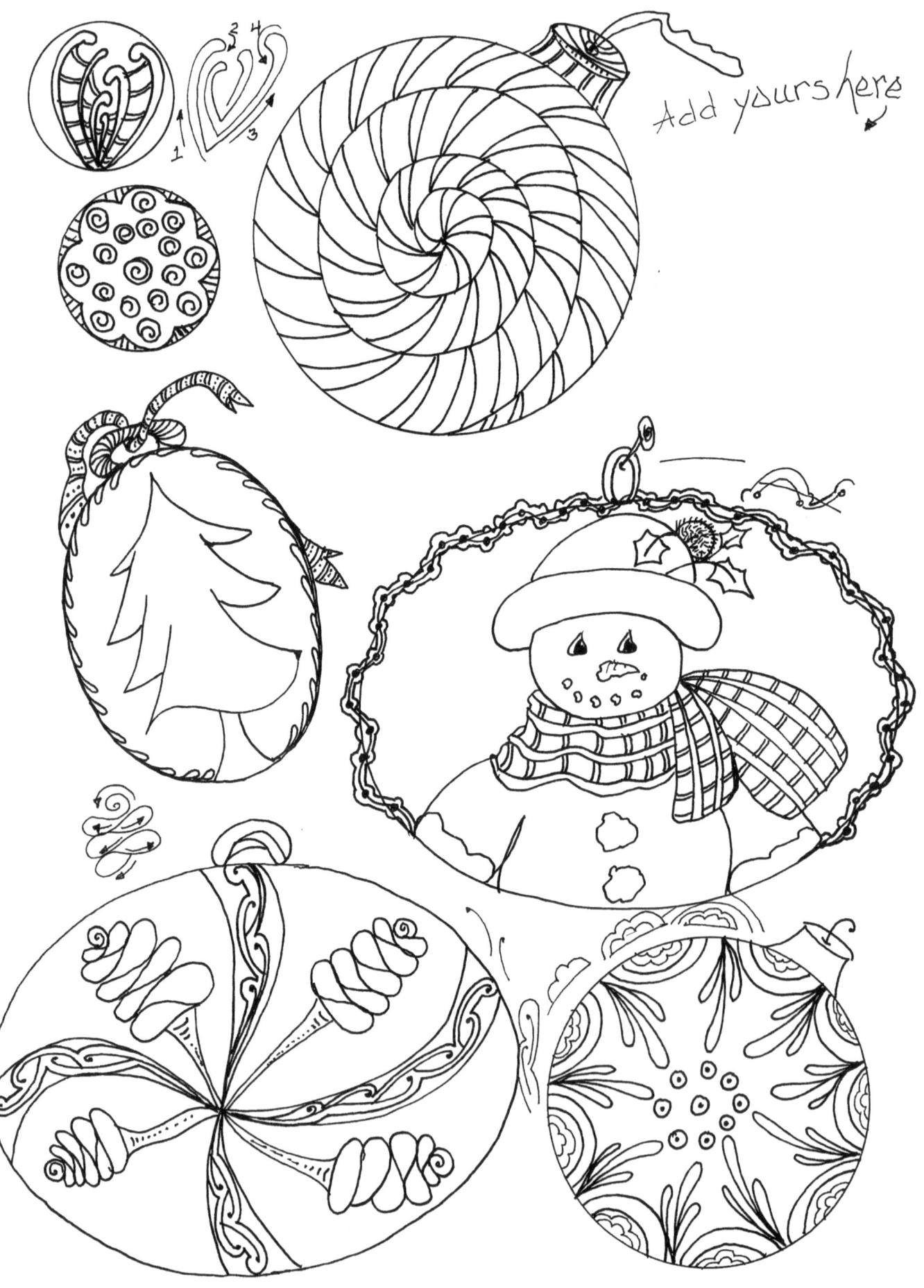

Add yours here

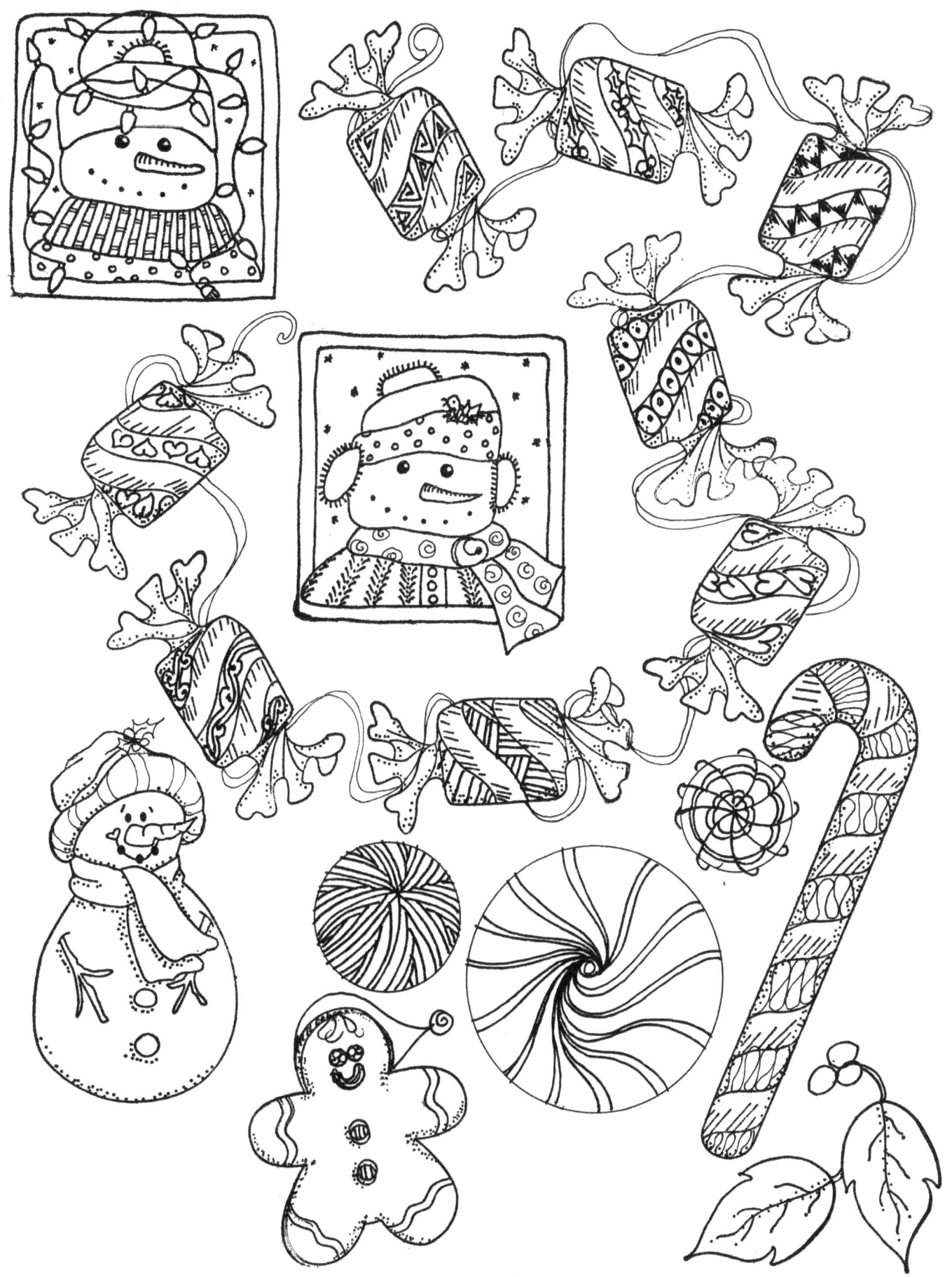

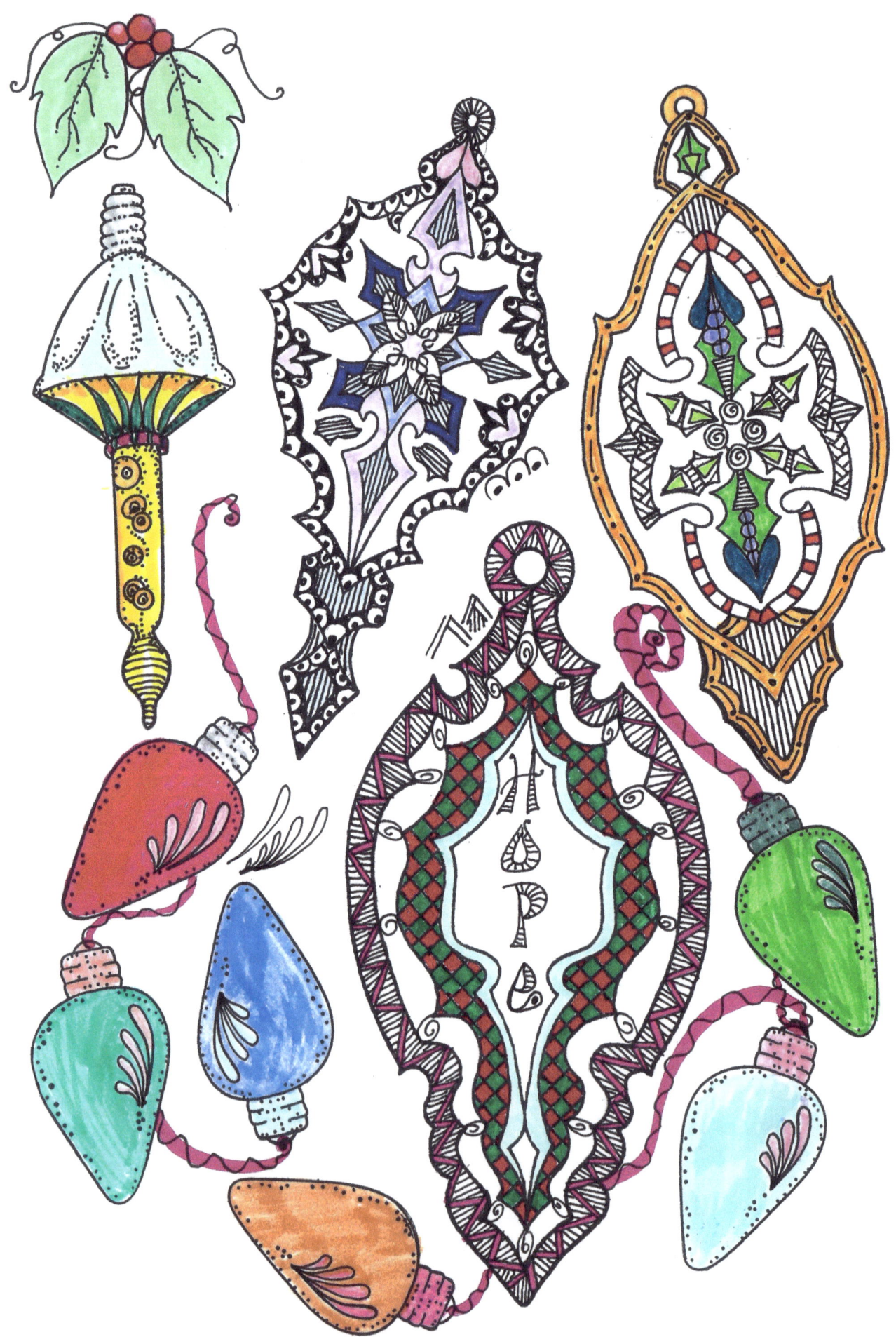

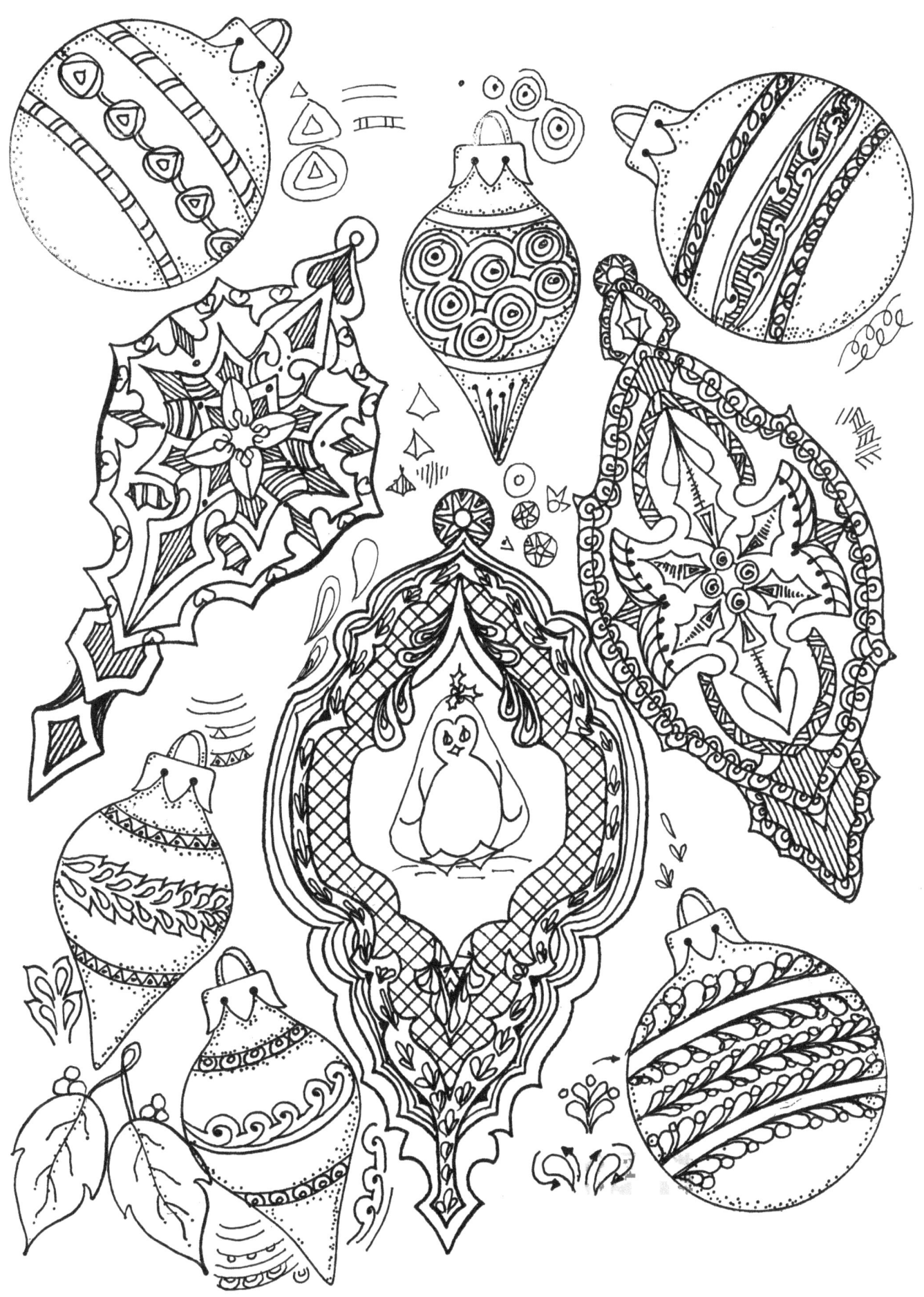

Ribboned Flakes

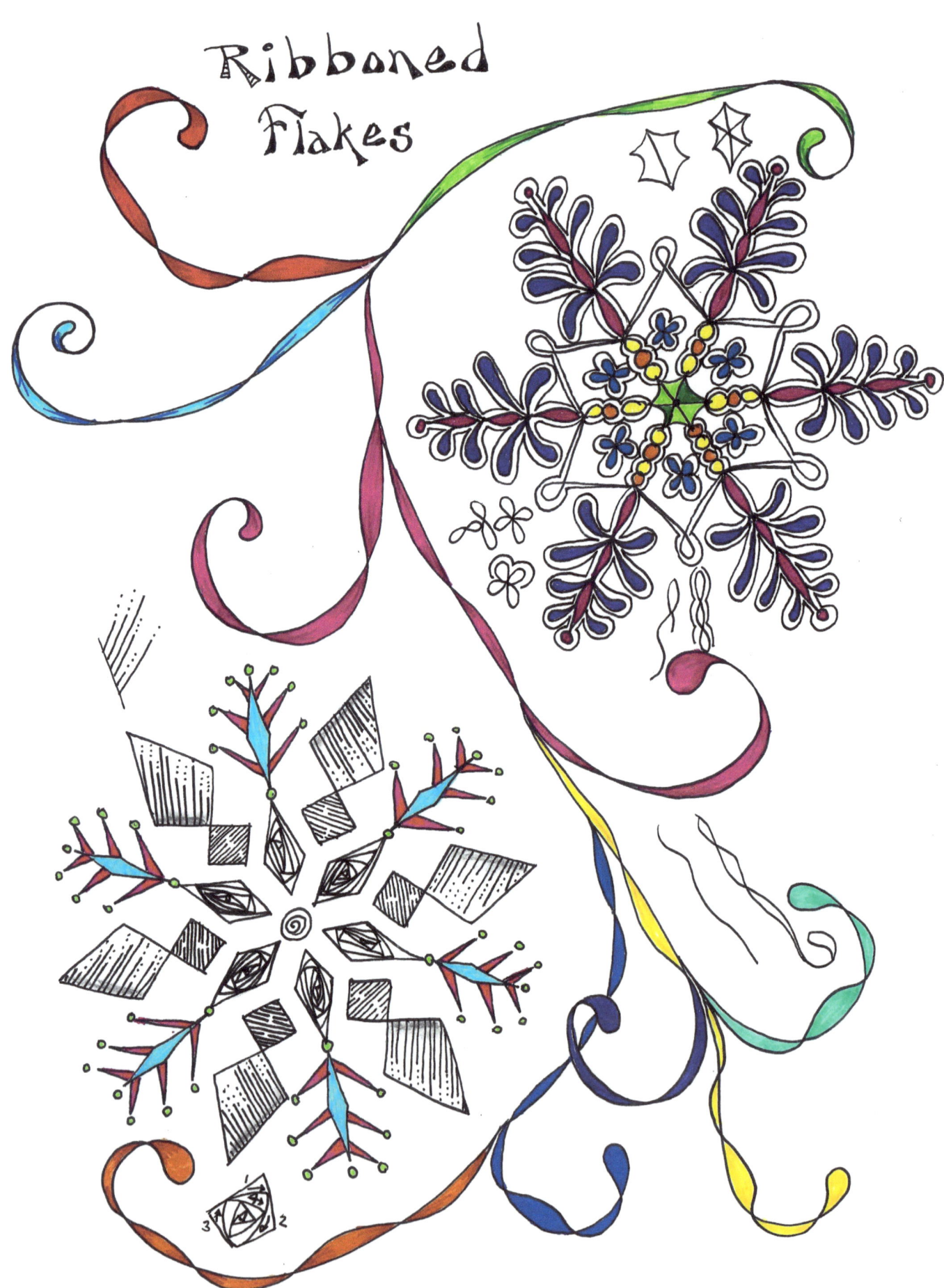

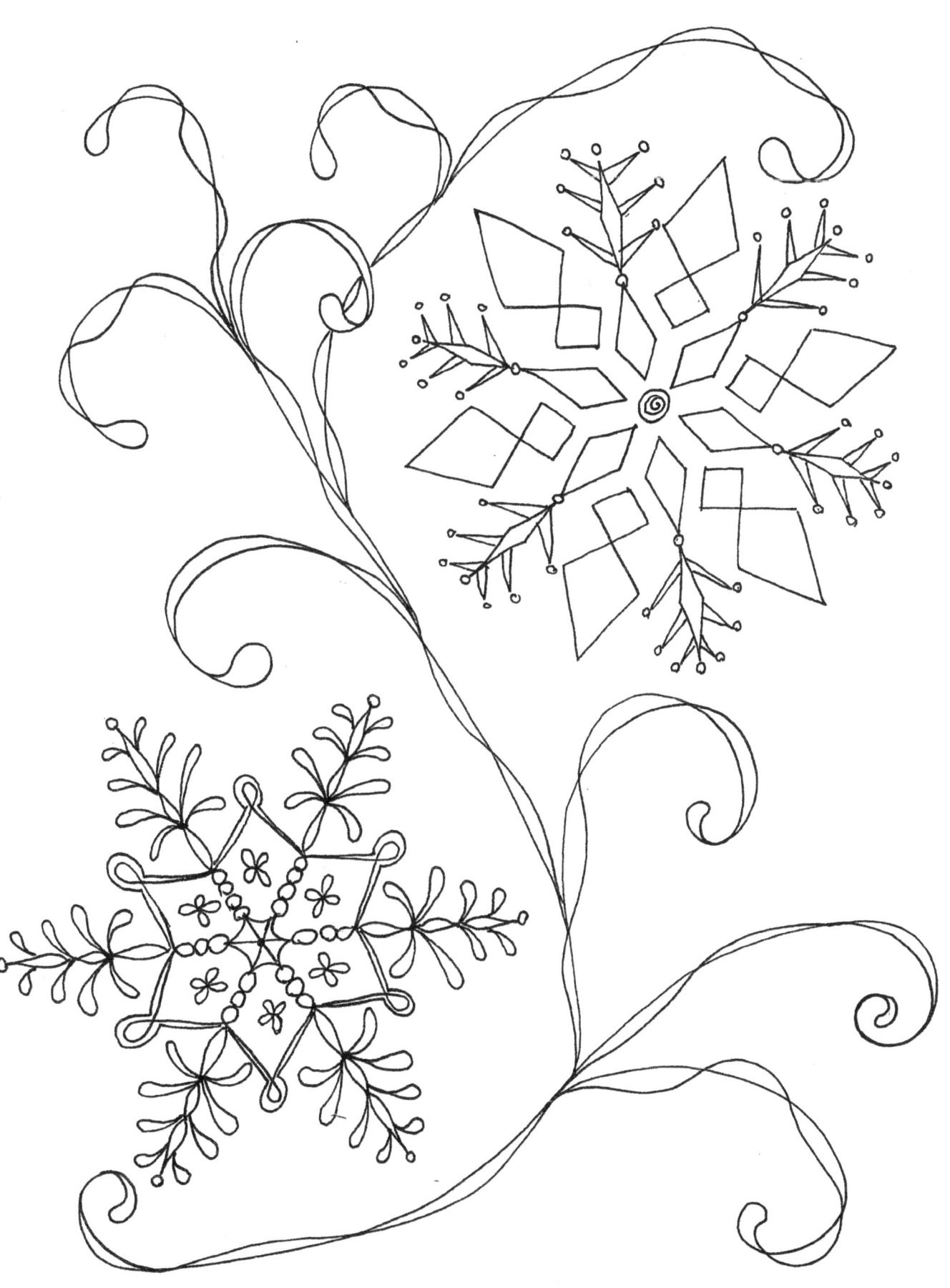

Happy Cats

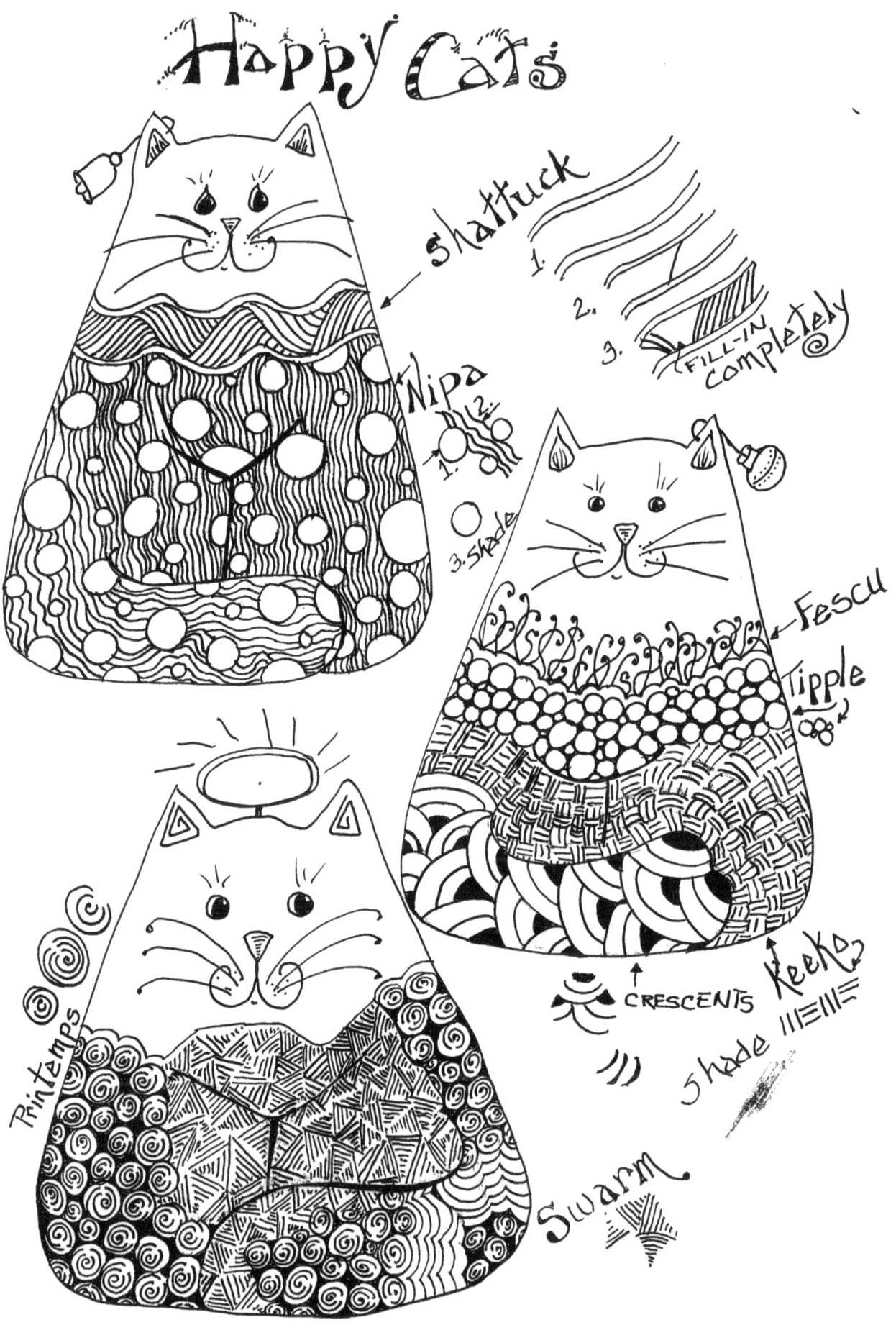

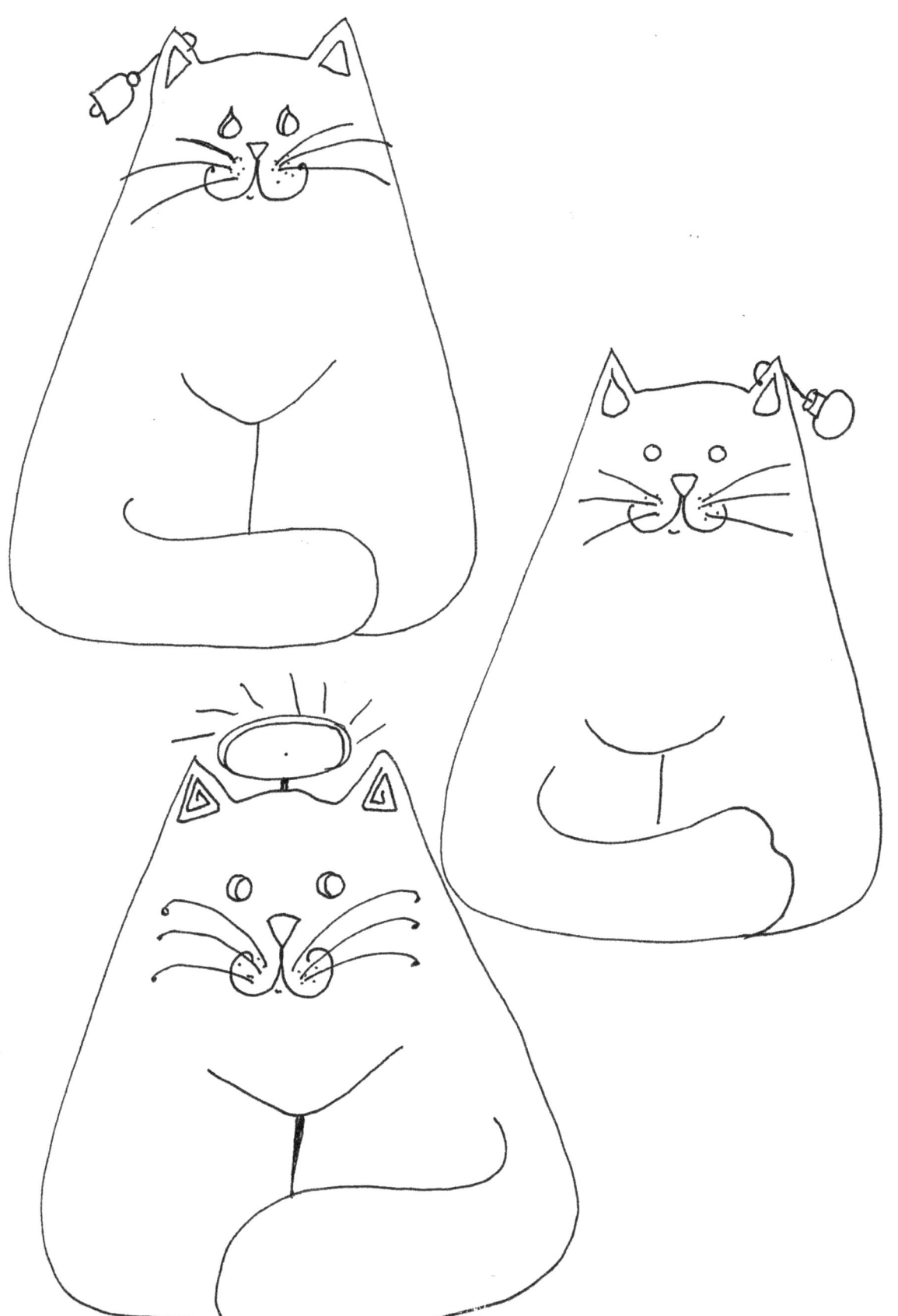

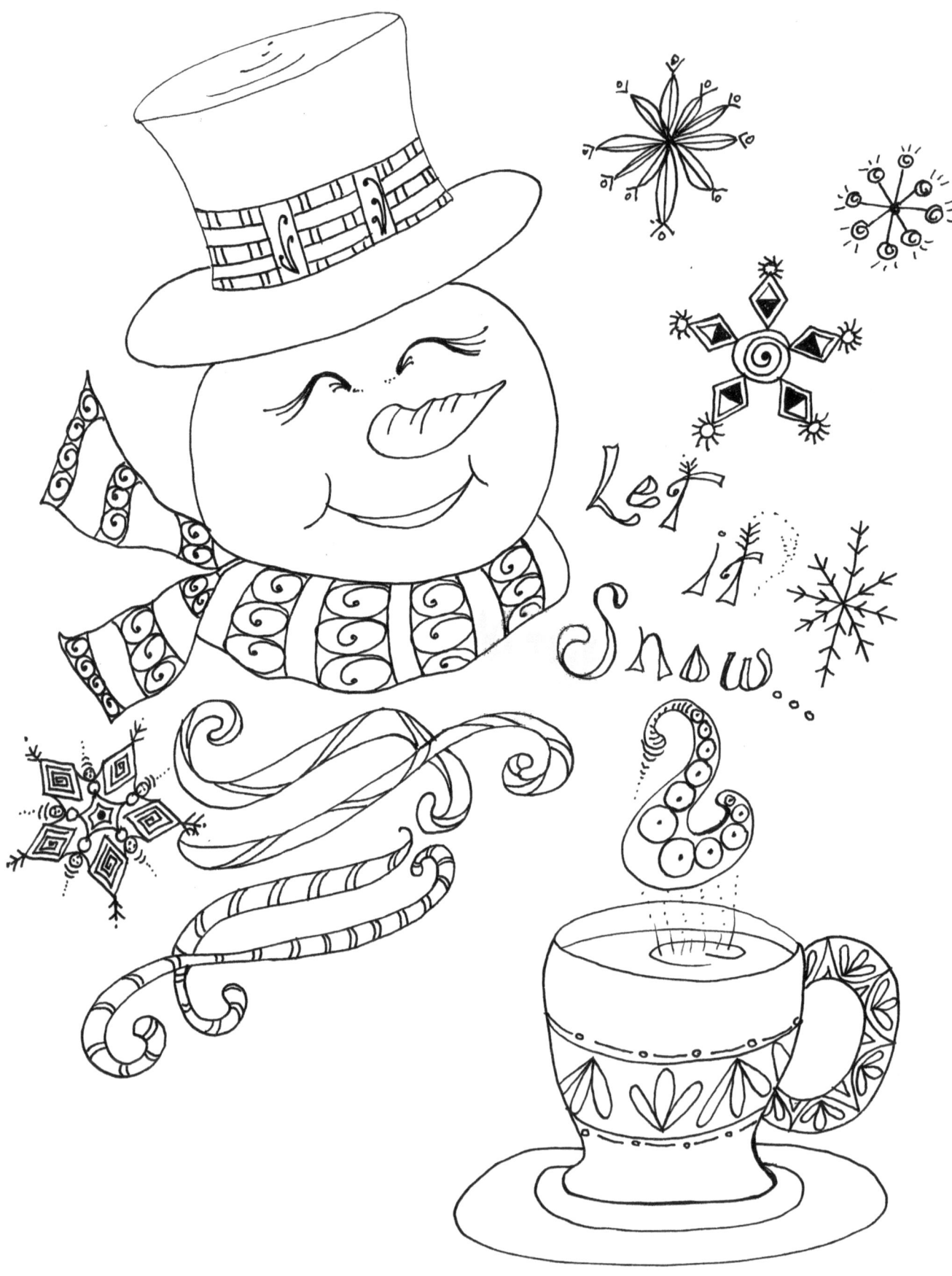

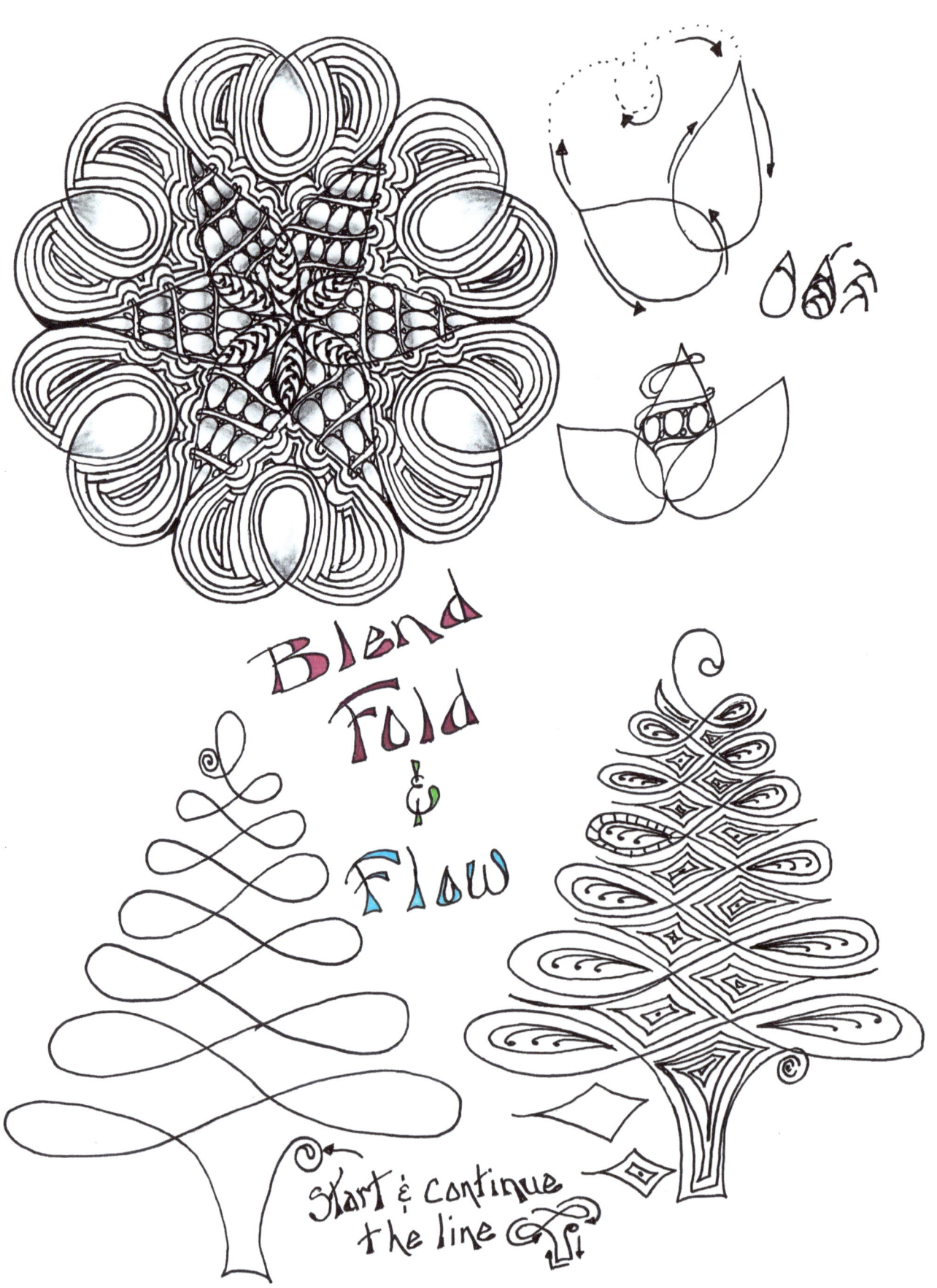

Blend
Fold
&
Flow

Start & continue
the line

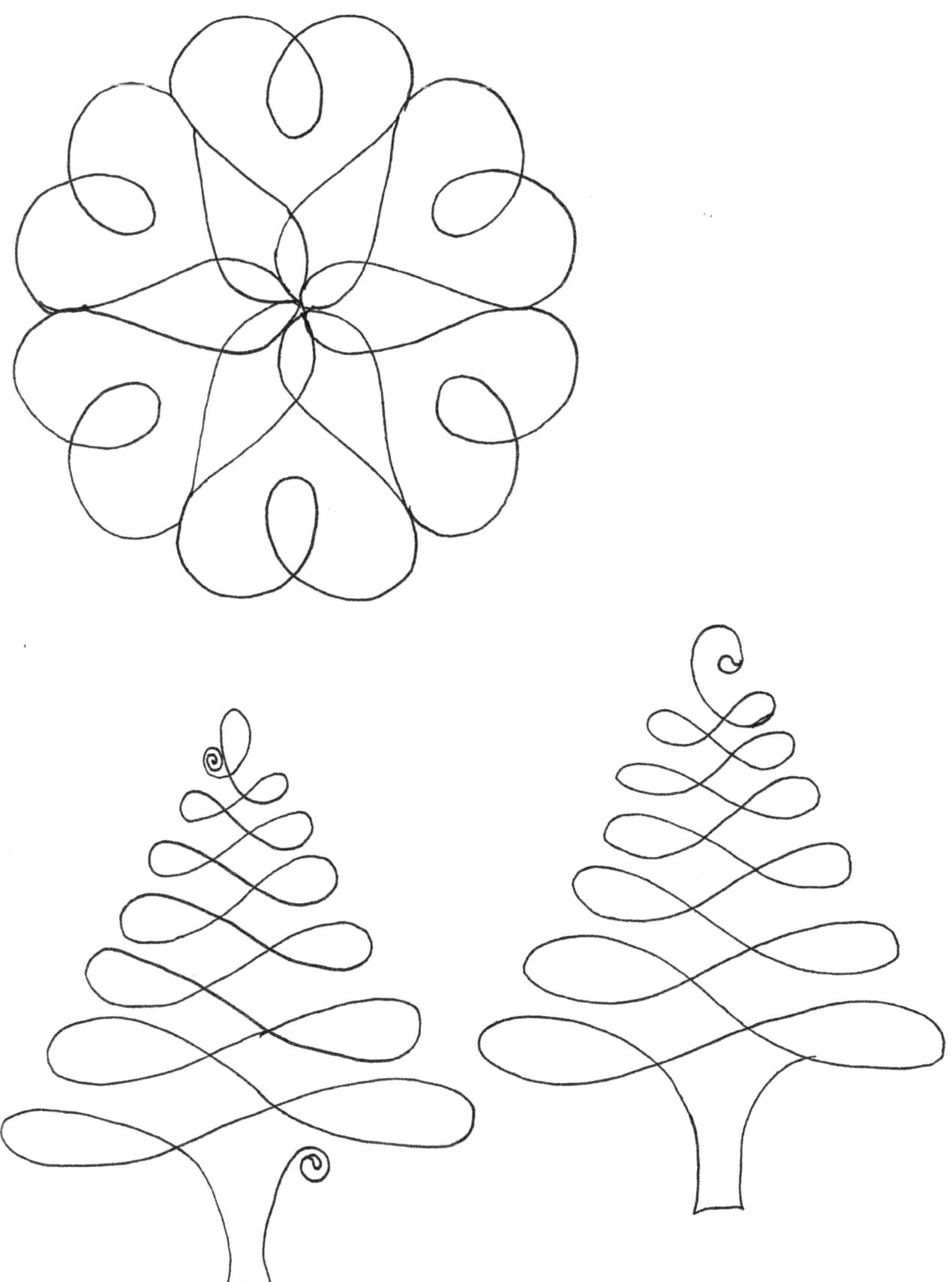

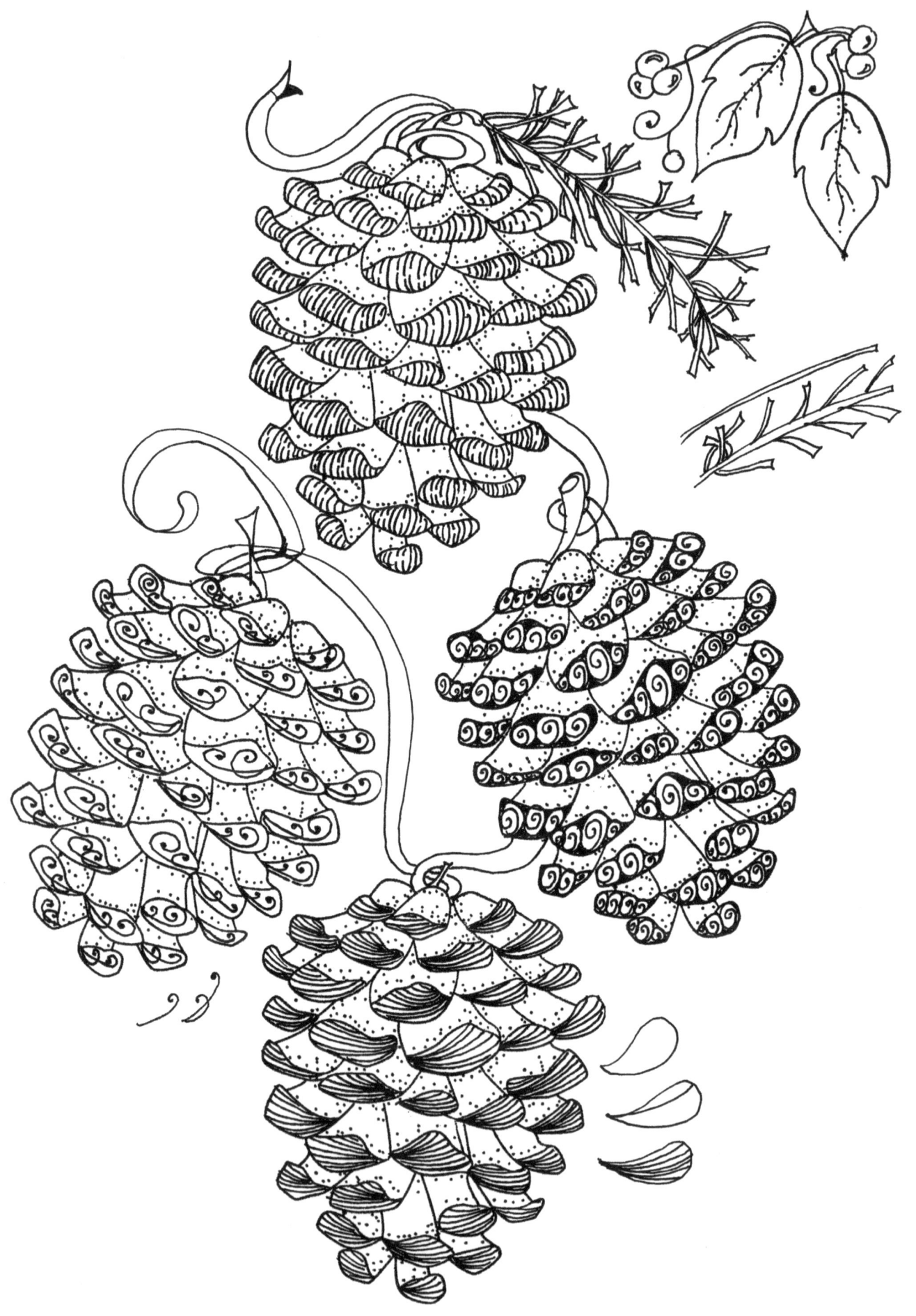

Sway

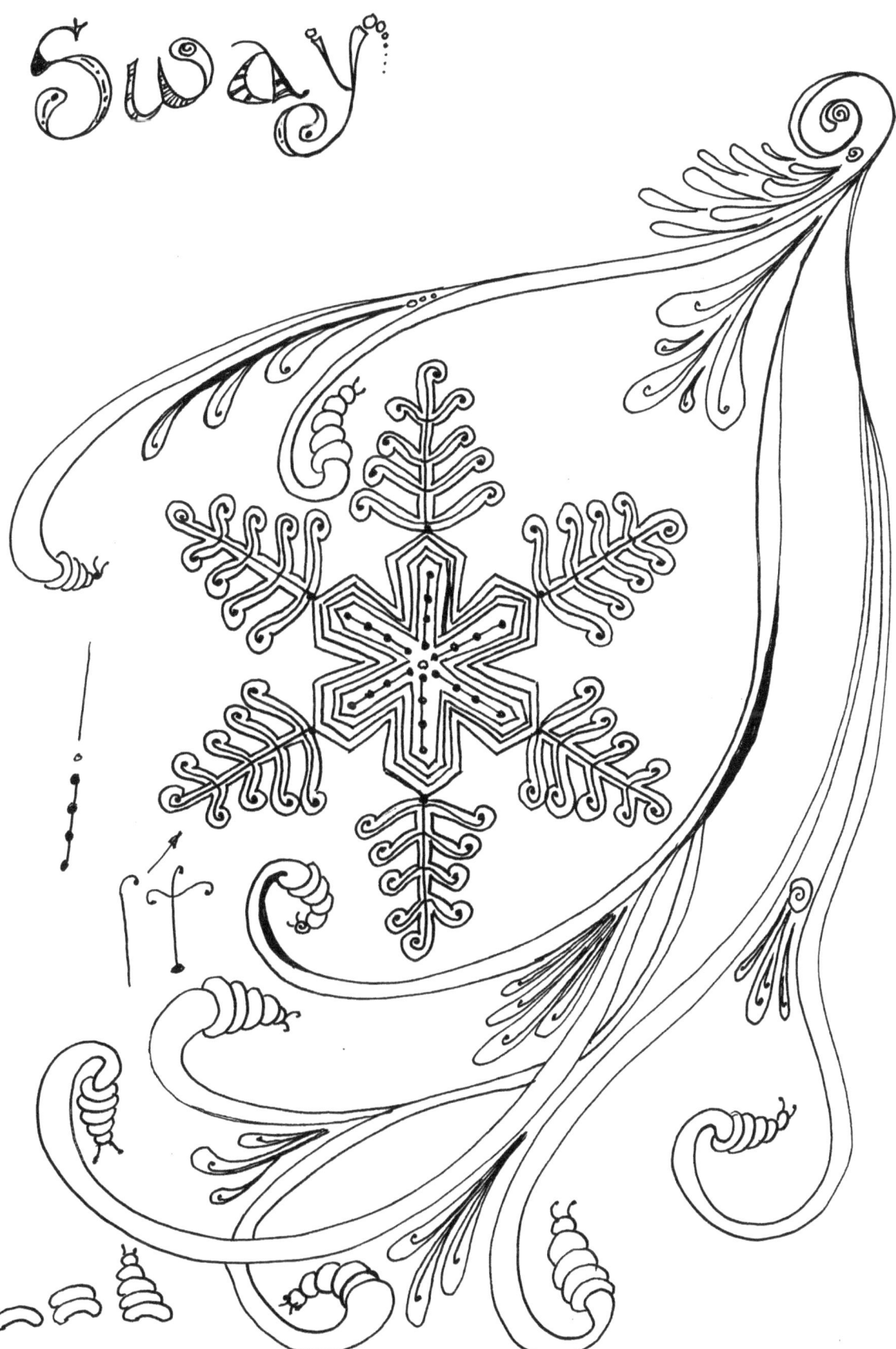

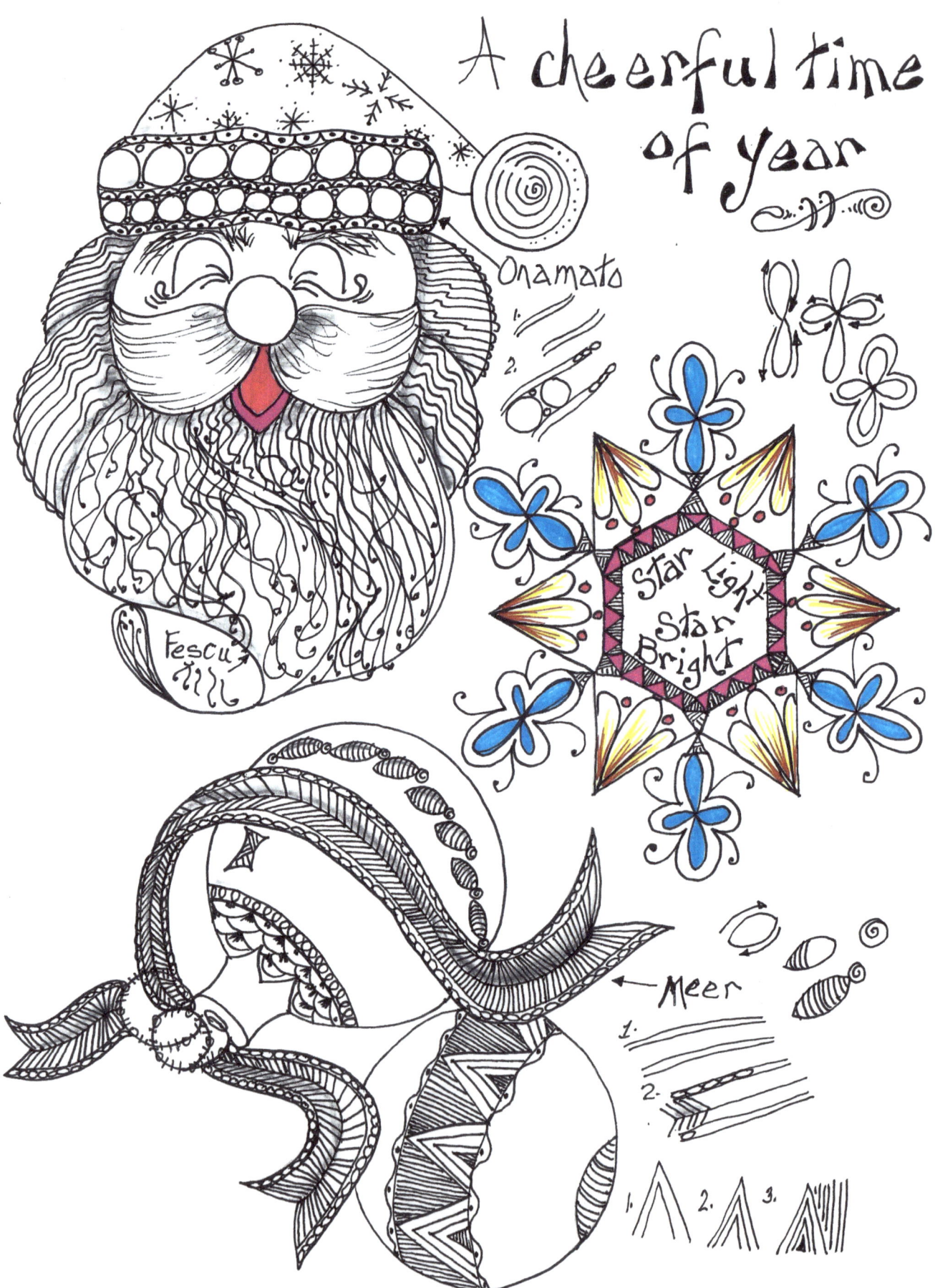

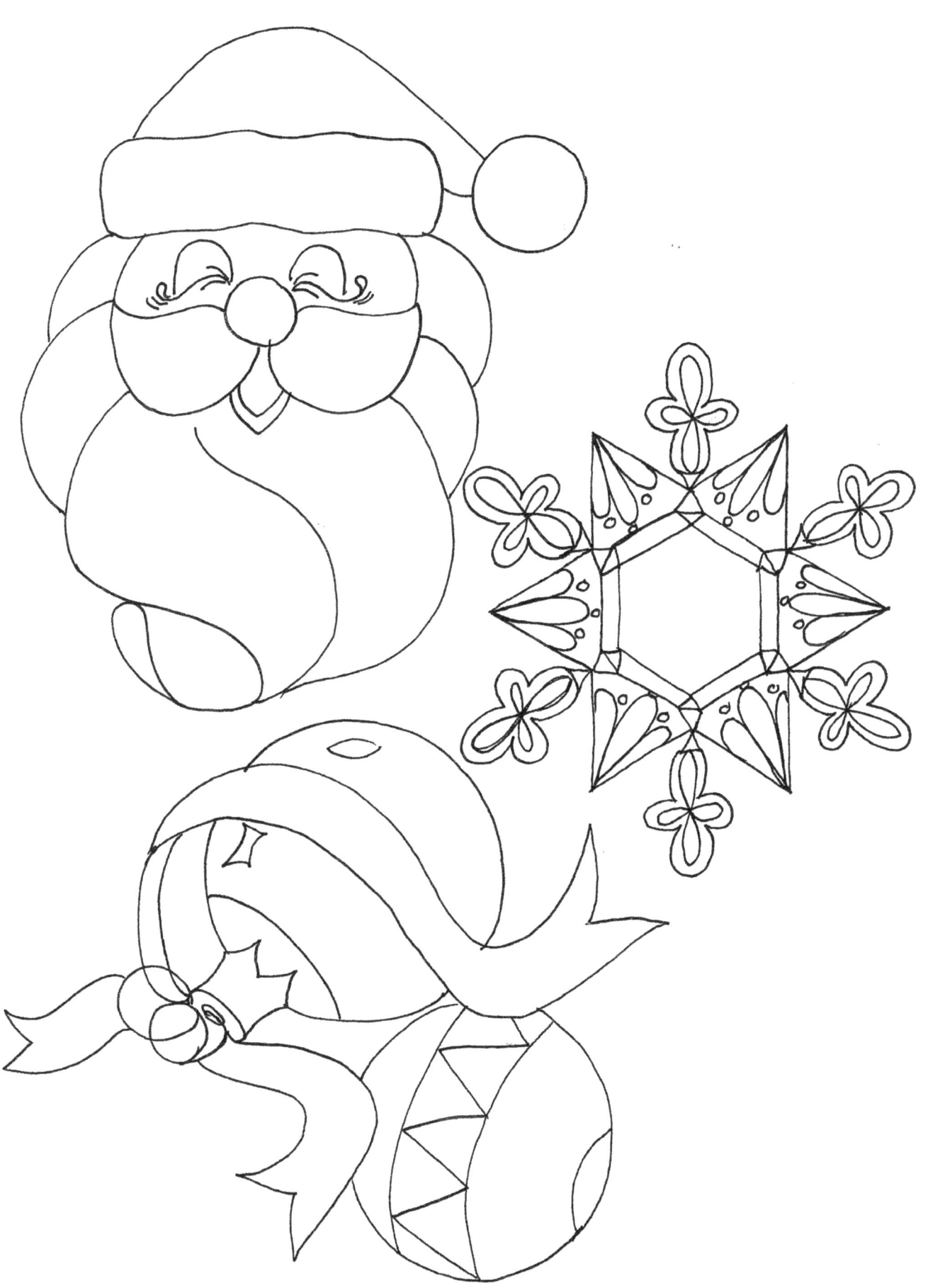

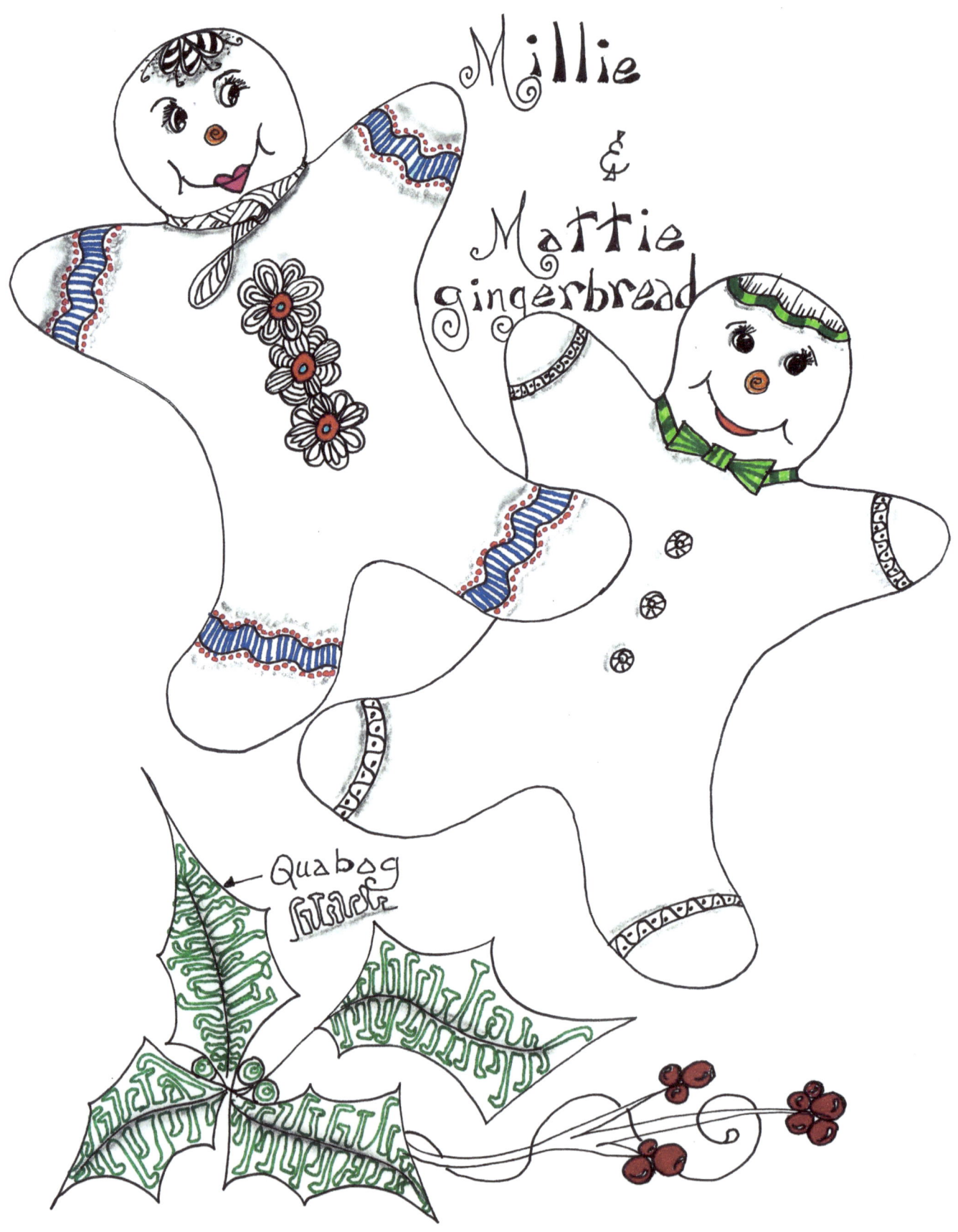

Millie
&
Mattie
gingerbread

Quabog
Black

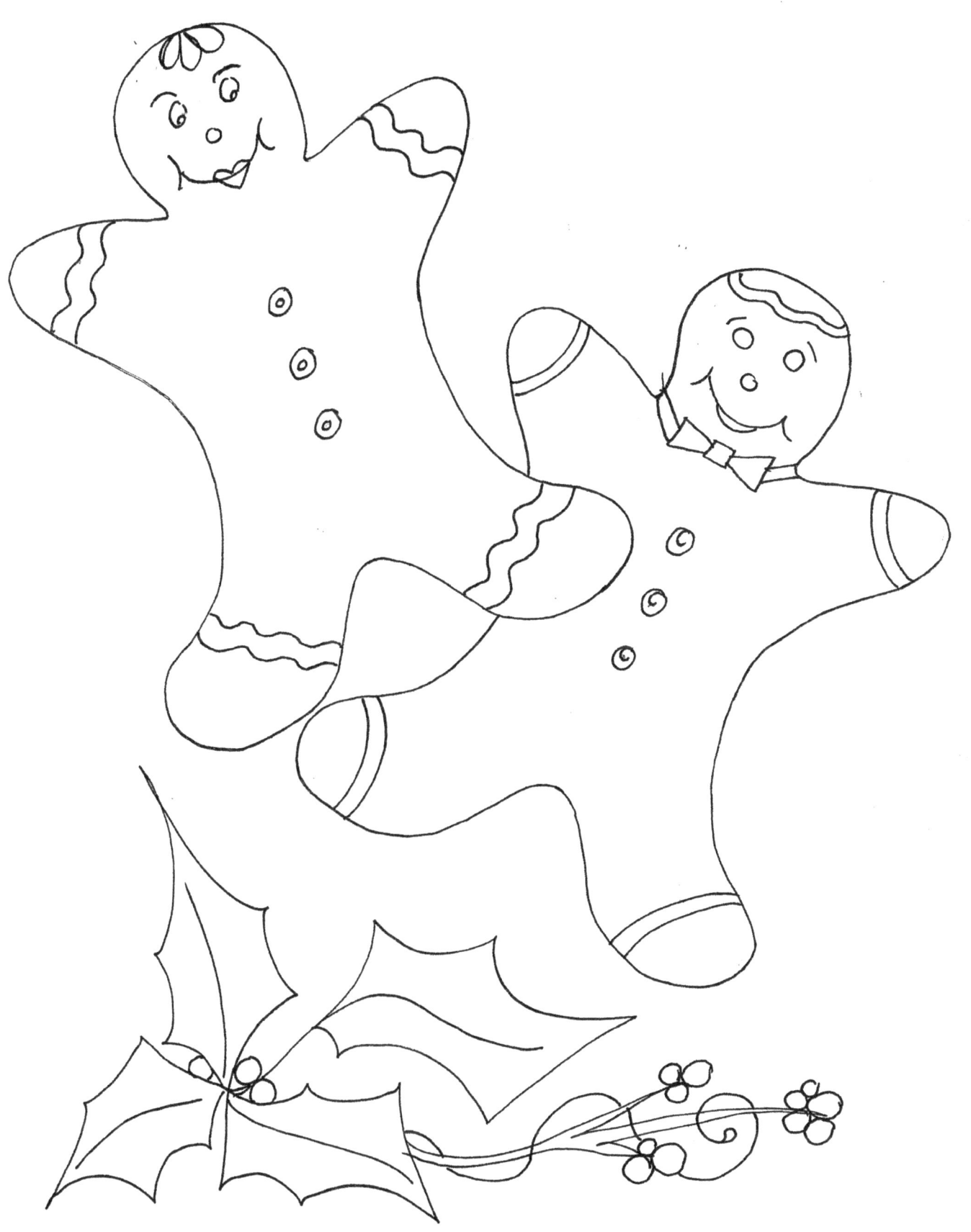

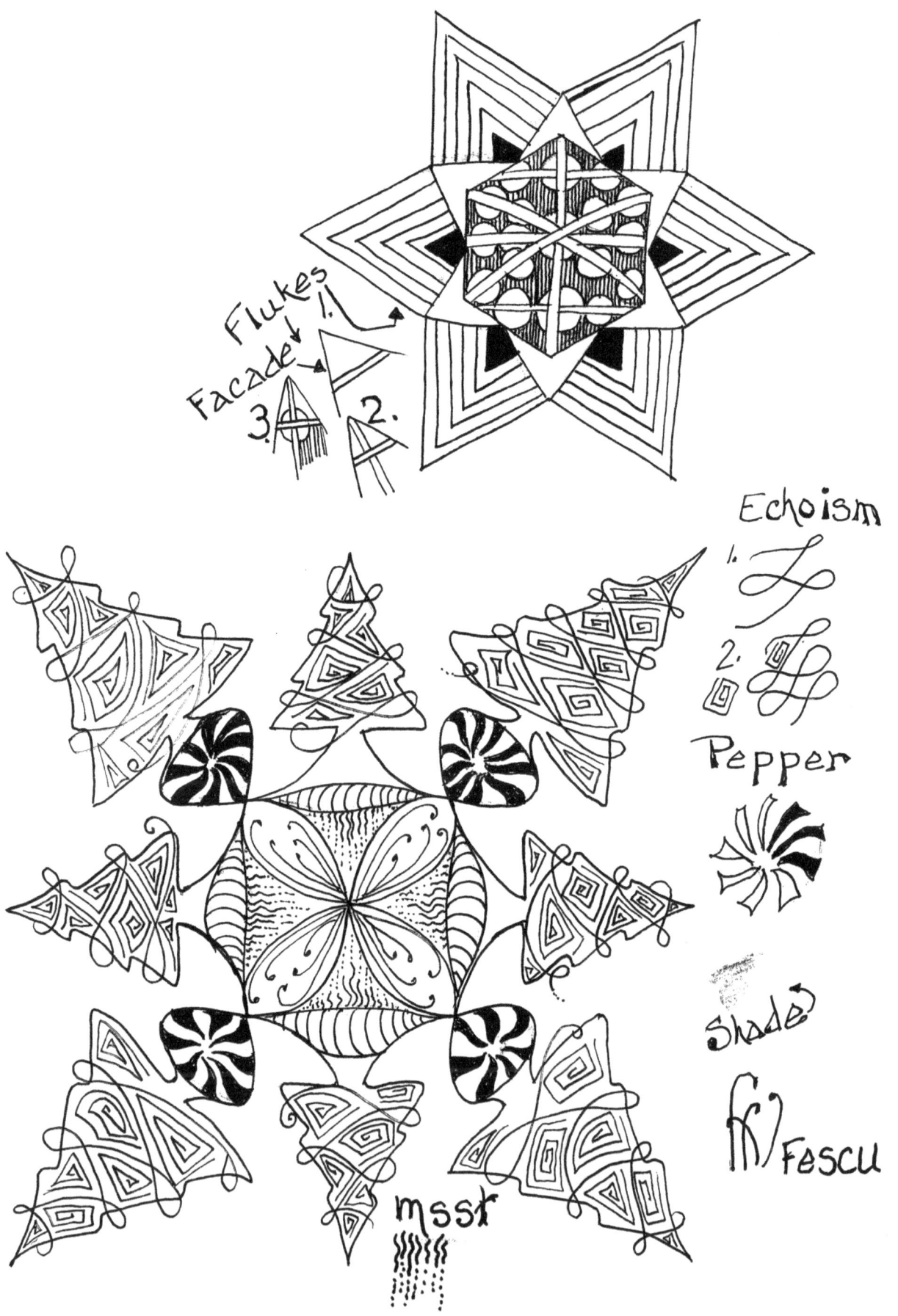

Flukes

Facade

1.

2.

3.

Echoism

1.

2.

Pepper

Shade

Fescu

msst

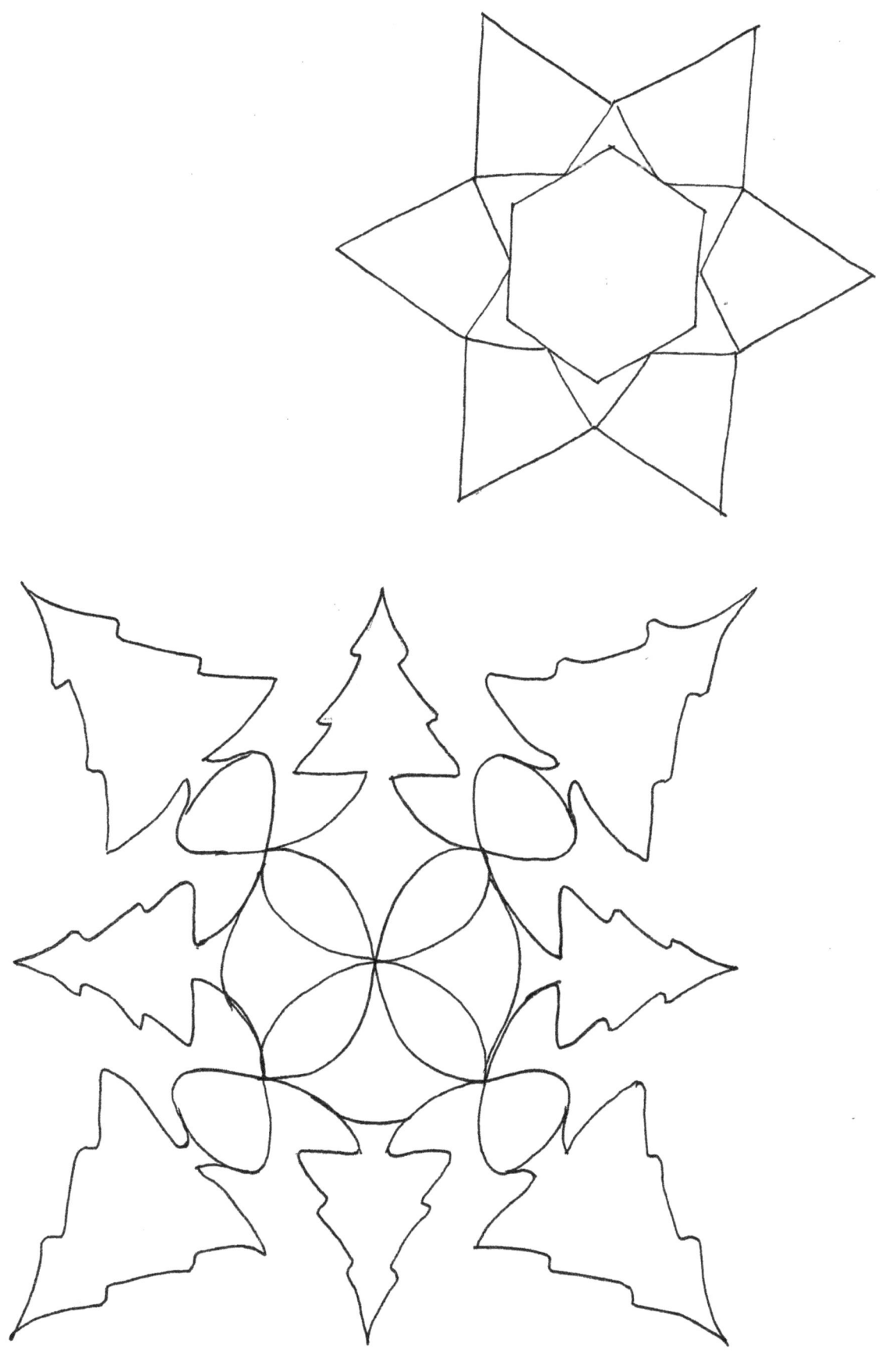

www.ingramcontent.com/pod-product-compliance
Lightning Source LLC
Chambersburg PA
CBHW040754200526
45159CB00025B/2089